"I have had the great privilege of having Márcia a[...]
more than three decades. The story of their life is [...]
and inspirational I know. They are true heroes in the fullest bibli[...]
they have made room for a remarkable God to do remarkable things through
them. This is a must-read book that will encourage and challenge you."

DAVID HAMILTON
Vice President for Strategic Innovation, University of the Nations

"I have been following the personal and missionary life of Suzuki and Márcia
for more than twenty years. I am a witness of how seriously they, still very young,
attended to God's call to dedicate their lives to the Brazilian indigenous peoples.
This book . . . displays the adventures of their walk of faith, their commitment
with the cause, and their courage to face obstacles of all kinds in order to see
the gospel shining in hearts that had been oppressed under dense darkness."

ROCINDES CORREA
*Coordinator, Departamento de Assuntos Indígenas da Associação das Missões
Transculturais Brasileiras (DAI-AMTB)*

"Márcia was destined to be a world changer! She started at age seventeen in the
Amazon, walking days through the jungle and saving the lives of children from
infanticide by the multitudes. This book will grip your heart, change your atti-
tudes, and give you an understanding of how you too can be a world changer."

LOREN CUNNINGHAM
Founder, Youth With A Mission

"This story will lead you not only through a fascinating life experience, but also
to the Lord's heart. It shows how the power of God can act in any environment,
bringing light and hope. Reading this book will help you understand other people's worldview, as well as help you to believe that in God everything is possible."

RONALDO LIDÓRIO
Missiologist, Presbyterian pastor, anthropologist, and writer

"An excellent book chronicling one Suruwahá child's amazing struggle for survival in the absolute madness of an infanticide culture. . . . Be deeply moved by
this harrowing account of minute-by-minute survival with an ultimate message of hope. My prayer is that as you read these stories . . . your own faith will
grow in the midst of whatever God has called you to, so that you will play your
part in helping to transform our world. Superb reading!"

WELLINGTON OLIVEIRA
President, YWAM Brazil

A WAY BEYOND DEATH

*A Brazilian Couple's Fight against
Fear, Suffering, and Infanticide*

JEMIMAH WRIGHT

YWAM PUBLISHING
Seattle, Washington

YWAM Publishing is the publishing ministry of Youth With A Mission (YWAM), an international missionary organization of Christians from many denominations dedicated to presenting Jesus Christ to this generation. To this end, YWAM has focused its efforts in three main areas: (1) training and equipping believers for their part in fulfilling the Great Commission (Matthew 28:19), (2) personal evangelism, and (3) mercy ministry (medical and relief work).

For a free catalog of books and materials, call (425) 771-1153 or (800) 922-2143. Visit us online at www.ywampublishing.com.

A Way Beyond Death: A Brazilian Couple's Fight against Fear, Suffering, and Infanticide
Copyright © 2012 by Jemimah Wright

Published by YWAM Publishing
a ministry of Youth With A Mission
PO Box 55787, Seattle, WA 98155-0787

Library of Congress Cataloging-in-Publication Data
Suzuki, Márcia.
    A way beyond death : a Brazilian couple's fight against fear, suffering, and infanticide / by Márcia Suzuki as told to Jemimah Wright.
        p. cm.
    ISBN 978-1-57658-430-9
        1. Indians of South America—Missions—Brazil. 2. Indians of South America—Brazil—Religion. 3. Indians of South America—Brazil—Social conditions. 4. Missionaries—Brazil—Biography. 5. Suzuki, Márcia. 6. Suzuki, Edson. I. Wright, Jemimah. II. Title.
    F2519.3.M5S89 2012
    299.8'981—dc23   2012000872

Cover photo of the Suzuki family appears copyright © 2011 by Brooke Valle.

With the exception of one name that has been changed to protect identity, all of the content in this book is factual.

Unless otherwise noted, verses marked NIV are taken from the Holy Bible, New International Version®. Copyright© 1973, 1978, 1984 by International Bible Society. Used by permission of Zondervan. All rights reserved.

First printing 2012

Printed in the United States of America

Men, women, and children of every culture on earth deserve the right to life. As missionary linguists studying tribal languages and cultures, my husband, Suzuki, and I have spent our lives helping indigenous tribes of the Amazon fight for this right. Here is our story, in my own words, as told to journalist and author Jemimah Wright.

This book is dedicated to my loving family: my mother, my father, my husband Suzuki, my beautiful daughter Hakani, and the indigenous peoples of Brazil.

MÁRCIA SUZUKI

International Adventures

Sateré Song

Atiky'e eku'uro hap
Mi'i tag ahenoi at kaap,
Atiky'e earia yp posok
Uimowaku eku'uro hap.

I love all Your death represents.
I will talk about it until the sun sets.
I love the scars of the nails in Your hands.
Your death enables me to be beautiful, holy, and acceptable.

Contents

Foreword

I WAS DEEPLY MOVED by this book. That might be partly because I am a friend of the main people in the story. Márcia and Suzuki have been my friends and colleagues for decades now. I trust and respect them deeply, having known them during the events that are described here. They are trustworthy, devoted followers of Jesus. They are also brilliant linguists and understand the diversity of human cultures and aspirations as expressed through language.

This is a powerful story. It's a story of identity, as Márcia and Suzuki discover Jesus—their inclusion in Him, in His family, and in His plans for humanity. It is a love story, as Márcia and Suzuki find each other, are married, and pursue the purpose of their lives together. It's a story of calling, as the couple struggles with great difficulties in order to define, pursue, and persevere in God's plan.

It is also a story of loving sacrifice, as Márcia and Suzuki leave all of the conveniences and the relative safety of modern life behind in order to love and help isolated peoples. It's a story of family, as Márcia and Suzuki save and adopt a little girl condemned to death. And it's a story of forgotten peoples—Amazonian tribes struggling to deal with the steamroller of technological civilization as it inexorably advances toward their homelands.

This is a story of startling reciprocity, as Márcia and Suzuki learn deep truths about Jesus from the Suruwahá people. This tribe's interaction with our living God, out of their unique worldview, produces profoundly moving insights that have blessed Márcia and Suzuki and can now bless you.

Most of all, this is a story of divine initiative and inclusion. God pursues tiny tribes through servants willing to go to the ends of the earth. He is not willing that any should perish, but wants everyone to come to Him. There is no tribe too small. There is no child too tiny and insignificant. He is pursuing them all to love them and to bring them to Himself.

This is a war story, as light and truth confront deadly lies. And it's a story of rescue: Jesus arrives to help a people tottering on the brink of culturally precipitated extinction, revealing Himself to them and pulling them back from the edge of the abyss.

More than anything, this is a story of God's unrelenting love for all peoples. Márcia and Suzuki are central characters here, but the power and the love don't come from them. God is the source and the initiator. He doesn't stay on the sidelines as a conveniently controllable theory. As Márcia and Suzuki respond to Him, Jesus gets dynamically involved. There are deep revelations and inspiring miracles.

If you are serious about knowing our living God more deeply, if you are fascinated by His commitment to even the smallest individual and the smallest child, if you want new insights into God's character and ways, if you seek beauty and understanding in the diversity of human experience and the insights that come when God interacts with isolated cultures, this book will help you. It will change you forever.

JIM STIER
Field Director of the Americas, Youth With A Mission

Prologue: Healing in the Amazon

DUSK WAS FALLING in the Amazon clearing, but the heat had not abated. The moisture-infused air still buzzed with insects and the sounds of crickets, birds, and frogs calling in our vast tropical surroundings.

Heading for my hammock, I moved under the thatched roof of the large round longhouse hut, known as an *uda*, which was home to the entire Suruwahá tribe. The noises of wildlife were immediately replaced by the sounds of people cutting firewood, women crushing corn, and children playing. The uda was so big and well constructed it seemed like a marvel of practical engineering. Each family had their own area in this great, open space.

It was 1993, and my husband Suzuki and I had lived with the Suruwahá Indians off and on for several years. The Suruwahá live in the middle of the dense rainforest, at least two weeks travel from modern civilization.

That evening the atmosphere was tense, as one of the women had an infected tooth and was crying out in pain, her face already swollen from the infection. Suzuki called me over to try and help her, when suddenly Ikiji, one of the men in the tribe, came running to us. He was panicked and crying.

"What is it?" Suzuki asked, standing up to comfort the young warrior.

"My wife, Siraki, she is dying. I gave her your pills but they didn't work," he cried. Scrambling to our feet, Suzuki and I followed him to where Siraki was lying in her hammock.

We had recently given Ikiji treatment for malaria, but it was dangerous for his wife to take the pills as she was heavily pregnant. Kneeling down by her side, I could just make out her face from the flicker of the burning embers in the fire close by. Her eyes were closed, and her body was shivering with fever.

I put my hand on her forehead. She was burning up, and it looked very much like she was suffering from malaria. What worried me most was that the medicine her husband had given her could potentially cause her to miscarry. As if confirming my fears, Siraki's mother, who had been at her side the whole time, suddenly cried out, "The baby is not moving! It is dead!"

Slowly in a high, moaning tone, she began to chant a song of mourning for the baby.

I put my hand on Siraki's swollen womb; it was still, with no sign of life inside.

Suzuki and I were both praying when Siraki's mother suddenly urged Suzuki to "blow" on her daughter, like the shamans do. The Suruwahá knew that Suzuki liked to sing, and their shamans would get possessed by spirits when singing in the jungle. They mistook Suzuki's worship to Jesus as a sign that he too was a shaman.

Suzuki crouched down as the shamans do and cupped his hands around his mouth. He blew on Siraki, speaking to the fever to be gone in Jesus' name. At the same time, I was crying out to Jesus under my breath to save this girl and her baby for His glory.

Suddenly Suzuki looked up. "Is *zama hinijaru* a word?" he asked me.

"I don't recognize it, why?"

"I feel like I am supposed to speak it over her, but I don't know what it means," he said.

He asked Ikiji and Siraki's mother if they knew the word.

"Oh yes, it is like when there is a big storm and lots of noise, and suddenly it stops and there is peace and stillness. Or if someone has a lot of pain and then in an instant it goes, that is zama hinijaru," Ikiji said.

So Suzuki started to declare the words over Siraki. After a little while we put our hands on her belly, and she didn't feel hot anymore. Then suddenly I felt the baby move.

"Zama hinijaru," Siraki said all of a sudden as she opened her eyes.

Siraki's mother and Ikiji could not believe what they were seeing; they started cheering and shouting. Siraki had been completely healed and her baby was alive. Suzuki and I made our way back to our hammocks, thanking God for answering our prayers.

A few days later the Suruwahá asked Suzuki whom he was talking to when he blew on Siraki.

"It must have been a very powerful spirit," they said with respect.

Suzuki then explained that it was Jesus, the Son of the Living God.

"Who is this Jesus? Is He strong? Does He know how to hunt? Please bring Him to us so we can eat with Him," they asked. Suzuki tried to explain that he could not bring Jesus to the uda, because He was not a person like us.

At this point we did not have enough vocabulary or cultural knowledge to explain more. We would just give vague responses or would tell them that we were going to explain later. We were immersed in studying the myths and worldview of the Suruwahá because we needed to find the correct terms to introduce Jesus. Otherwise we would give room to religious syncretism (blending two beliefs) in the tribe.

Suzuki and I knew we had to wait to introduce Jesus, but what the Suruwahá didn't know was that He was already there.

PART ONE

Early Life

A Stick in the Fire

LOOKING OUT of our bedroom window on a hot summer's morning, my sister Margaret and I watched our neighbors, the Jardim family, pile into a van and drive off down the road.

"They look so excited. Where are they going?" Margaret said.

"To church," I replied knowingly. At seven I was one year older than Margaret. I liked to show her that I was wiser too.

My family lived in an apartment block in Rio de Janeiro, Brazil. I had jealously watched my neighbors go to church each Sunday. My parents were not religious, so they never took us, but I longed to go. I imagined it would be lots of fun. After all, my neighbors looked so happy as they left each Sunday morning.

Suddenly I had a great idea.

"Let's ask them to take us with them," I said to Margaret.

So the next time Margaret and I saw our neighbor, I boldly asked if they would take us to church. They were surprised, but delighted, and agreed right away.

I knew that if I told my parents we had invited ourselves, they might not let us go, so I devised a plan.

"Mama, the neighbors have invited us to church," I lied. "Can we go?"

Mama agreed. She was brought up in the Assemblies of God Evangelical Church, and although she no longer attended, she felt it was a good thing.

The following Sunday I woke up early in great excitement. Margaret and I were ready long before it was time to go. I put on my best dress and tied ribbons in my hair. I wanted to look good for God.

We arrived at the Methodist church and followed the other children to Sunday school. A beautiful woman began telling us a story about what Jesus had done on the cross. My heart was captured. I hung on her every word. At the end of the talk, the teacher asked if anybody wanted to accept Jesus into their lives. I had no doubts. I had heard the message and understood it. I wanted Jesus in my heart.

So that Sunday morning, at the age of seven, Jesus became my Lord. Excitedly I went home to tell my parents what had happened. My mother seemed pleased but my dad was uninterested. He thought church was a waste of time, but harmless enough for me as I was only a child.

My father, Daniel dos Santos, was a self-made man. He came to Rio at seventeen, from a family of farmers in a northeastern Brazilian town. He hadn't learned to read or write, but he was ambitious and traveled to Rio to make something of himself, working by day and studying by night. He married my mother Vanda, and they went on to have five children: Marcos, me, Margaret, Maryangela, and Daniel. My father was always studying when we were children. By day he would work as a policeman to feed and clothe us, and by night he studied law at the university. We all had to pitch in and help because he was often exhausted. Papa would record his lectures and then we would listen and make notes for him. When he graduated and became a lawyer in his thirties, there was much celebrating as we all knew how hard he had worked for it. I loved and respected my father but was sad he wasn't interested in my churchgoing activities.

When I was ten, I heard about missionaries for the first time. Someone who had been a missionary came to preach at church. My little heart soared with excitement.

"I want to be a missionary," I exclaimed to my parents when I got home. There was a distinct lack of interest and approval. But I was young, and surely it was just a passing phase, they must have hoped.

The next year there was a big Bible quiz at church. It was mostly for the adults, but I had been studying and was allowed to join in. Each contestant sat at the front of the church and answered Bible questions. To my amazement, even as the youngest in the competition, I won. The prize was a weeklong trip to a Christian camp called Palavra da Vida. I was so happy; there couldn't have been a more appreciative winner.

The camp had a big impact on the rest of my life. There were many missionaries speaking, and their stories inspired me. One evening after the talk, there was a call for people who wanted to commit their lives to being missionaries and serving the Lord.

They built a huge fire, and every person who felt called took a stick or branch to add to the fire. I picked up my stick and walked to the fire, telling God I would go anywhere for Him. As I threw my stick into the fire and watched the flames get brighter and stronger, I realized then that I could make a difference even though I was young. I knew I wanted to serve the Lord.

In my excitement I came home and told my parents what I had done.

"That is ridiculous," my father shouted. "What kind of a life is being a missionary? It's for people who don't work, not for *my* daughter."

He was very upset, and I couldn't convince him to trust my decision. Our relationship was very affected, and I missed my father's closeness. However, I couldn't give up what I felt was a call to the mission field.

When I was fourteen I decided it was high time I got out there. I wrote to every missionary organization I had ever heard of, asking them if I could join. To my disappointment they all wrote back saying I was too young, that I should finish my studies and then contact them again. But then I heard of an organization called Youth With A

Mission (YWAM). Surely a mission with a name like that would take young people.

Finally! I thought as I wrote off asking to join.

But they too wrote back saying I was too young. I was very frustrated until they contacted me a little while later saying I could join them for a monthlong outreach over winter vacation. Even though by this time I was fifteen, and sixteen was the age required for the trip, they decided to give me a chance because I had been so insistent and written them so many letters begging to come.

With a group of thirty other young people, we went to a city in the Minas Gerais region of Brazil. It wasn't easy or comfortable. The girls slept in the damp cold basement of a church. Every morning we would wake up, and the wooden walls would be wet with humidity. We didn't have much money for food, but I didn't mind at all. I loved the whole experience; I was in my element telling people about Jesus, loving them, and showing them how much God loved them.

My plan was to join YWAM for a year after leaving school and take part in their Discipleship Training School (DTS). Before my first trip with YWAM I had thought of going to college to become a veterinarian, but after my missionary experience I changed my mind. I had found a new passion and calling.

So at seventeen I finished school and applied to do a DTS at the only YWAM base in Brazil at that time, in Contagem, near Belo Horizonte. Again I was a year too young for the course, but they made an exception and I was allowed to attend. While I was there God spoke to me about my future. For the first time I was hearing people talk about the Amazon Indians in the north of Brazil. Something about them touched me, and I felt God say they were the people He wanted me to go to. I also felt He said that my time with the Indians would be my university education.

I had always imagined that I would go to Africa or China, but now I knew that God was telling me to go to people in my own country. When I told my fellow students, everyone laughed. It seemed crazy; I was so young and no one had done anything like it before. At that time YWAM Brazil was only doing short-term missions; no one had gone long term to a people or place.

When I broke the news to my parents, my dad was dead set against it.

"You are making the worst mistake of your life—don't do it," he said adamantly.

He didn't talk to me for almost a year after I made the decision. I hated going against his wishes but was sure I was making the right choice.

I knew that I wanted to get to the Amazon—the largest rainforest in the world, with 1.4 billion acres belonging to nine nations, 60 percent of which is in Brazil—as soon as possible, but I didn't know how. YWAM didn't have anyone working with Indians. Then one day, while still at the DTS, I came across a magazine with an article about Wycliffe Bible Translators. They worked with different tribes and were offering a linguistics course.

That is what I want to do, I thought excitedly.

After applying I was accepted to the course, and in the summer of 1982 (this was January through March in Brazil), I began my three-month Wycliffe training in Brasília, the capital city of Brazil. It was the first time I had studied linguistics, and I loved it—so much so that I advanced to the top of my class. The time flew by, and in the last week a Canadian couple named Fran and Harold Popovitch invited me to come with them to the Maxakalí, a tribe in the state of Minas Gerais. The Popovitches had been missionaries with Wycliffe for many years, and they were now starting a literacy program among the Maxakalí.

I couldn't contain my excitement. At last I was going to be a missionary to the Indians. But when I arrived in May of that year, I was deeply saddened. The Maxakalí were often drunk and would fight and try to kill each other. Countless times I had to get in the middle of a fight to split up the sparring Indians. Harold Popovitch gave me basic instructions on the Maxakalí language, but for the most part I was on my own.

I lived in a house in the Maxakalí village with a group of students from a Minas Gerais university. They were part of a program run by the anthropology department, trying to help the Maxakalí overcome their alcohol problems. My job was to teach the Indians to read and write in their own language.

I had no financial support the whole time I was with the tribe. My mother sent money, but there had been a problem with the bank and it never arrived. Each day I prayed in faith, asking God to provide. I knew He could, and I didn't understand why it wasn't happening.

"Where is your God now?" laughed the other students, making fun of me.

I cried every day, but held on to my faith. I was allowed to receive meals with the other students, as I promised to pay them back, but I had no idea how the money would come. It was the hardest test to learn to obey God even when He did not give me what I wanted, when I wanted it.

One evening as I was on my knees crying out to Him, I felt He spoke to my heart:

After this time you will never have problems with money again.

My faith was deepened and strengthened in those three months as I waited for God to come through. From then on I never doubted God in this area. On the last day a Christian anthropologist from the university came to visit the students. When she heard from the other students that I had no money, she paid all my expenses in full.

My heart melted when I found out what had happened. I praised God, who fulfilled His promises to me. That was one victory, but there would be more heartache.

One Sunday afternoon I spent some time with an Indian woman. We ate baked sweet potato outside her hut and laughed together, trying to understand each other through the language barrier. She had three small children and was heavily pregnant with the fourth. Her husband had walked four hours to Santa Helena, the nearest large village, to try and sell handcrafts. The Indian men would do this most weekends to get money for alcohol. If they couldn't sell their wares, they took them to the bar and exchanged them for beer. The wives were always worried for their husbands when they went out, as there was a strong chance they might not come back alive. The tribe was self-destructing. They were getting into fights and killing each other.

After a while, I left my Indian friend and headed home. Her husband still hadn't come back. She was so worried that she went out to search for him in the middle of the night, walking the path in the pitch blackness, her children sleeping back in the hut.

The next morning some of the Indians came running to our house saying she and her baby were dead.

Please, God, may it not be true, I prayed under my breath, but I knew deep down that she was dead. I tried to ignore the growing feeling of panic as I went with two other students in the tractor to find her.

After forty minutes we found her body. She was naked and black and blue from bruising and bites. Her baby had been stillborn and had human bites all over his little body. Some of the Maxakalí had walked to where she was. A small group stood around her, each one of our hearts breaking at the injustice. We were all so shocked. I couldn't stop the tears from falling, I felt so desperate, completely helpless.

Later her husband admitted he had gotten angry and attacked her. He had murdered his wife, but there was no punishment for him.

It wasn't only the Indians whose lives were in danger. On the weekends the other students and I had to bar ourselves into our house as ten to twenty Indians would come completely drunk in the middle of the night and try to get in, wanting to rape us. Thankfully they never did. But because of this stressful environment, two of the female university students had breakdowns. Another student who had been three months pregnant miscarried the baby after seeing what had happened to the woman who had been killed by her husband.

I was the only Christian in the house, so I would pray continually, sometimes out loud. It was a baptism of fire into the Indian culture, but God supernaturally increased my heart and love for the people. I was crying as I said goodbye to the tribe after three months. I didn't want to leave, but I felt God was telling me to go to the Amazon.

As I prayed, God had given me pictures of a tribe by a waterway of rivers, surrounded by thick jungle. I saw myself with the tribe, and I knew it was in the Amazon.

I told Gerson Ribeiro, a YWAM leader, about my dream of a tribe in the Amazon.

"Why don't you come back to YWAM and start a ministry among Indians?" he suggested.

The thought appealed to me even though Wycliffe had wanted me to stay with them. They had even generously offered to pay for all my schooling, a master's and a doctorate, as well as my housing. But I am a pioneer at heart, and I knew I wanted to go and start a new work with YWAM. A base had just been set up in Belém in the north of Brazil on the edge of the Amazon. I joined the team there that July and began helping at the first YWAM linguistics course. All the while, as I was getting myself prepared, God was preparing a tribe for me.

Deep in the Jungle:
The Sateré-Mawé

THAT TRIBE was the Sateré-Mawé. Their chief, a man named Kadete, realized that his people were destroying themselves through alcohol and fighting each other, just like the Maxakalí were. As their leader, he felt the burden of responsibility for his people. But nothing he did seemed to make any difference. Kadete knew he was supposed to be a guide and chief to his people, but he did not know what to do. Finally he had had enough; he could not stand by and watch his tribe self-destruct. He decided to abandon his Sateré-Mawé tribe and move to a city.

Kadete took a canoe and traveled to Manaus, located in Amazonas, the largest state in Brazil. There he got drunk, was beaten up and robbed, and became destitute. However, despite being homeless he had a quiet dignity about him. He still had the presence of a chief, even though he had left his people and was living in poverty.

After several years in Manaus, Kadete was walking in a poor neighborhood when he was attracted by the sound of singing coming from a building nearby. He went to take a closer look and walked into a small church service.

The homeless Indian was a strange sight among the worshippers. Kadete took a seat near the back and started to listen. He had picked up a bit of Portuguese and understood the gospel message that was being preached.

Suddenly he became excited.

"This is *Tupana* that you are talking about!" he exclaimed. Tupana was the Sateré-Mawé name for God. Kadete knew Tupana, but this was the first time he had heard of Him as a loving God.

When the pastor asked who wanted to give their lives to Jesus, Kadete went straight to the front. Later Kadete described his salvation experience as "Jesus hanging His hammock in his liver." To the Sateré-Mawé, the liver is like the heart is to us—the place of emotions—and when you hang your hammock somewhere, it means you are there to stay. He was saying Jesus had come to stay in his heart.

On hearing the good news, Kadete had a deep desire to go back to his tribe and tell them what he had heard. At last he had a message of hope for his people. Tupana would deliver them from alcohol. Tupana would help them.

It took Kadete several months to get back to his people, but when he started to preach they wouldn't listen. He tried for days to explain the gospel, but the results were the same. His people would not listen.

Eventually, in desperation, Kadete decided the only way was for him to go back to the church in Manaus and ask them to help him. He made the long return journey to the church.

"Please come to my people and tell them about Jesus," he pleaded with the pastor.

"I have work to do here, but perhaps someone else will go," the pastor said.

The invitation was given to the church, but no one in the whole congregation was willing. Kadete would not give up. He persuaded someone to write a letter for him to send to other churches in Brazil.

"Someone must come," he implored.

The letter, written in Kadete's name, stated that he was the chief of his Sateré-Mawé village in the Amazon. It asked for someone to come and live with the tribe and teach them about Jesus.

"Don't worry about food or where you will stay," dictated Kadete. "I will build you a house and hunt for your food and give you *manioc*." Manioc is a starchy root high in carbohydrates, a staple food in the tropics.

The letter was written and sent from church to church, congregation to congregation. Kadete excitedly went back to his people to prepare a place for the missionaries. He built a beautiful new hut for them and planted manioc and sugar cane for them to eat.

But the weeks went by, then months, then years. No one came.

Every day Kadete would pray, "Lord, please send someone." But there seemed to be no answer.

The beautiful hut became old and started to fall apart, and the people laughed at Kadete's insistence that someone would come to tell them good news.

By this time, the letter that was still circulating around churches was old and tattered. One of the pastors who received it decided to make copies and send it out again.

One of these copies made it to a missionary conference in the south of Brazil. The YWAM Belém leader, Gerson Ribeiro, was there. When he heard the letter read, he felt God speak to him. As he got up to preach to the people, he told them that he knew a missionary who would go to the Sateré-Mawé. He was thinking of me.

When he spoke, God's Spirit fell over the place. One man stood up and offered his brand new motorbike as a gift toward sending a missionary to the Sateré-Mawé. After he pledged his bike, the floodgates opened, and many were moved to give gifts of money, even the jewelry they were wearing, to help send the first missionary to Kadete's tribe.

A week or so later Gerson came back to the YWAM base in Belém. He took me and another girl, Euci Cabeço, to dinner and told us the story. I knew when I heard about Kadete that this was the tribe God had been preparing me for.

Later that night I lay on my bed praising God, tears coming to my eyes in happy emotion. I was so excited at the prospect of meeting the Sateré-Mawé and telling them about Jesus.

That spring (September 1982) I journeyed deep into the Amazon jungle with Euci, Gerson, and another YWAM leader, Josué. For five days we traveled in a very comfortable tourist boat. It was huge, and we felt like we were on holiday. We then transferred to a smaller boat, not quite so luxurious and full of gold miners, for the second part of the journey. One evening over dinner I asked one of the miners to pass me the jug of what I thought was delicious cashew juice. Everyone laughed; it wasn't juice but water from the river, still brown and dirty. I couldn't drink it. When we reached the Amazonian city of Maués, we got into a large canoe with a roof and outboard motor for the forty-eight hour trip to the Sateré-Mawé.

My heart was so excited to be nearing the Indians. The final part of the trip in the canoe was breathtaking. The water was a deep dark blue, and I felt as if I were in paradise. As we neared the tribe, the river widened into a lake and I could see the thatched huts of the village, called Atuka, in the distance. In the sky over the village was a huge rainbow. All four of us got on the roof of the canoe and spontaneously started praising God for getting us there and for the beauty of His creation. We had our hands in the air and were dancing in excitement and praise.

When we arrived, the Atuka villagers were very warm and welcoming. Kadete was so touched we had come that he couldn't speak. The Indians fed us roasted monkey the first night. I was too tired and hungry to think deeply about what I was eating, but the young boys had fun explaining what the meat was.

A couple of years later I heard a story from one of the Sateré-Mawé women named Isabel. Before we arrived she had been having problems with her family. Her sons were always drunk, and her husband had sold their daughter to *asiagpot'u haria* (outsiders) to pay off a debt. Isabel was so depressed she was thinking of suicide. One night she had a dream. In the dream she saw four angels laughing and dancing and praising God under a rainbow. When she woke up a spark of hope stayed with her. Maybe God would send someone to help.

The next day she was washing her clothes by the water's edge when she heard the putt-putt of a boat engine. She looked up and squinted her eyes to see our boat on the horizon. She saw the four of us dancing and shouting on the roof, with a rainbow over our heads in the sky. Immediately she remembered her dream and ran to the villagers.

"Come quickly, I saw these people in the night. God has sent His angels to us. We must treat them well," she shouted.

It was because of Isabel that our reception had been so warm.

Even though Kadete was overjoyed that at last missionaries had come, so many years had passed since he had written the letter that the house he had built for the missionaries had fallen apart. Instead he invited us to stay in his hut with his family.

Kadete's hut was one of the largest. It was rectangular, without walls, and had a large sloping thatched roof. Inside there was a small thatched partition behind which Kadete and his wife Marciana slept. Euci and I slept with the children in hammocks on the other side of the hut. There was one big fire in the center and another little one by Marciana's hammock. Monkey heads were kept smoking over the main fire. The children would grab a head when they were hungry and suck the contents from inside before placing the head back over the grill to smoke some more.

The sun shone through the cracks of the thatched hut as Euci and I woke from our first night with the Sateré-Mawé. Lying in my hammock I couldn't help but smile. At last I was here. My mind was full with plans on how to study the language and befriend the people. Gerson and Josué were leaving us in the morning; it would be just Euci, me, and the Sateré-Mawé.

I had already learned a little of the language through a Wycliffe missionary named Albert Graham. Albert was well into his sixties and had been working with another Sateré-Mawé tribe in Pará, the second largest state in Brazil. He and his wife Susan had translated the New Testament into the Sateré-Mawé language. They had also recorded the Indians singing worship songs.

The Sateré-Mawé have a sacred and very old paddle. They believe the commands God gave them to live well are written on the paddle. But as years went by the people sinned, and in sinning lost the ability to read the commandments. When Wycliffe missionaries first got to the tribe and began translating the Ten Commandments from the Bible, the Sateré-Mawé excitedly brought them the paddle.

"These are the words written that we had forgotten. You are showing us the way again," they said.

After a day or two of getting used to living in a jungle village, Euci and I decided to introduce ourselves to the tribe. The village was set around a large lake in the river. There were about eighteen thatched huts dotted around the shoreline, with canoes moored at each house. We took our canoe and went from house to house, inviting the people to a service that evening in Kadete's hut. We also wrote down the names of the families in each hut. The process took the whole day, and Euci and I were starving at the end of it. We had expected to be fed, but at each hut, either they had just eaten, or there was no food. When we got back to Kadete's hut we just had time to bathe in the river before people gathered for the service.

As the sun was setting behind the jungle, the people started to arrive. They brought their hammocks and hung them on the beams around Kadete's house to sit on. There must have been about fifty people. I watched their faces, dimly lit by a few kerosene lamps, and my heart was filled with love for them. Mothers were softly rocking their babies off to sleep as they lay in the hammocks, but the children weren't sleeping. Everyone wanted to hear what the city people were going to say.

We had brought a tape player with us, so we started by playing some of the recorded worship songs from the Sateré-Mawé tribe in Pará state. They all loved the music and sang along as they learned the songs. I then tried to read from the translated New Testament. When I looked up from the pages I could see the faces staring at me intently, trying to follow what I was saying. If I stumbled over a word, they would shout out the right pronunciation to help me. After a while we went back to the singing. The service went well into the night, but eventually people started to leave, and Euci and I were able to fall into our hammocks, exhausted. I was still famished.

"Márcia, we haven't eaten anything all day. Are you hungry?" Euci whispered.

"Yes!"

"Let's pray. Maybe God will give us something."

I agreed, not really believing anything would happen. But as she finished praying Marciana called to us from behind the partition.

"Márcia, Euci—are you hungry? I saved some food for you," she said.

We both jumped out of our hammocks, amazed at the speedy answer to our prayer.

There was a fire underneath Marciana's hammock where she was warming the food. She told us it was a specialty, something really delicious. She hadn't wanted to give it to us when all the people were here, in case we didn't get enough. My mouth was watering thinking about what it could be.

There were two bowls over the fire. Marciana showed us the first one, with fresh wild mushrooms from the jungle, and then she opened the second one. It was full of large red ants. They had been drowned in water and had to be eaten raw. I tried not to retch.

I looked at Euci in horror, trying to suppress the wave of nausea that came over me. I couldn't believe it. Ants!

In my heart I started complaining to God.

"We asked for food and You give us *ants*?" I grumbled.

Almost immediately a voice came back: *If you want something else to eat you can leave. There are plenty of pizzas in Rio.*

I was instantly convicted. I had longed to come to these people and had been praying for them for years, and now I was complaining about the food. That was the last time I complained. Over time I learned to agree with the Sateré-Mawé that the raw ants are a delicacy. They are delicious and taste a little like mint. Now, thankfully, the days of waiting for food were past. The tribe started sharing everything with us.

After three months with the tribe, I had learned the language sufficiently to start explaining the gospel to the people. They were very receptive and so hungry to hear all we had to teach them. The whole village, bar a few men, asked Jesus into their lives. They stopped getting drunk and fighting each other. The transformation was amazing. They also told us about other Sateré-Mawé tribes upriver who, according to them, were very bad people. Euci and I started praying and felt a desire to visit them.

One day we had a visit from an Indian named Tomé, a Christian from a nearby village. He had heard there were missionaries and wanted to meet us, bringing a pumpkin as a gift. We talked to Tomé about our desire to go to other villages. He told us about Jovito, a pastor from Manaus who preached in the Sateré-Mawé village of Monjuru once a month. Tomé told us to come to his hut, six hours upriver, in a couple of days, and Pastor Jovito would be passing and could give us a lift to Monjuru.

When we told Kadete about our plans, he tried to put us off.

"They are bad people. They will be hostile to you," he said.

We told Kadete we had to go anyway and a few days later made the trip to Tomé's hut. Pastor Jovito picked us up, saying he would take us but that we shouldn't stay there because it was not safe. Daisy, Kadete's eight-year-old daughter, came with us. Her older sister was married to the son of the chief of Monjuru, and she wanted to see her. Kadete believed she would be safe.

The trip to Monjuru was breathtakingly beautiful. I wasn't paddling and could just take in the beauty. The water was dark, like cola but clear. Freshwater dolphins followed us, jumping around our boat. I saw macaw and parrots in the trees. It was stunning. The river went from being so wide that you could hardly see the other bank to very narrow. Eventually we arrived at Monjuru, where the sides of the riverbank were very steep, and steps had been carved into the mud—there were over two hundred steps up to the village.

Euci and I went straight to talk to the chief. We knew we had to ask his permission to stay longer than the three days with Pastor Jovito.

After asking where the chief lived, we were directed to the largest hut situated in the middle of the village. It was very similar to the Atuka village, with a thatched roof and no walls. We ducked to enter the chief's hut and came face-to-face with him.

The people called him *Tuxaua Sapo*, which means Frog Chief. He was tall, with darker skin than most Sateré-Mawé. He had short hair and wore clothes. The people in Monjuru looked very similar to any other riverbank community. The only difference was that the Indian women bathed naked, whereas the riverbank women were more modest.

"Can we stay with your people?" I asked Tuxaua Sapo.

"No, we never have white people staying here. You cannot stay," he said. (To the Indians, anyone outside the tribe is considered "white.")

Tuxaua Sapo was very stern and intimidating. At the time, I did not know that villagers believed the chief had powers of enchantment and could go to women in the night and exploit them sexually. The women would have no recollection of what happened when they awoke the next morning.

Still, I was safe here. It was culturally appropriate for any visitor to be welcomed and protected at the house of the chief.

Most Sateré-Mawé are hostile toward people outside the tribe because of the history of torture and abuse that has come from outsiders' hands. The tribe was first contacted by the outside world in 1669. In 1692 the Portuguese colonial government declared war against the tribe, and the hostilities continued until 1835 when the Sateré-Mawé clans joined together to fight them. But they were not successful. Men were paid by the government to hunt and kill the Indians and bring their ears as proof of the murder. Hunters or *bandeirantes* used to have necklaces with the ears of Sateré-Mawé Indians strung around their necks. The government wanted the Indians dead so they could take the land.

The Sateré-Mawé were successful warriors and often enlisted other tribes to help them fight, but it was not enough. They lost their lands and were made to live by smaller rivers in a different part of the jungle.

Sateré-Mawé boys have to go through an initiation ceremony to become men. Part of the ceremony is to wear gloves made with palm strings and macaw feathers filled with poisonous black bullet ants. The men dance and sing all night holding their gloved hands high, enduring intense pain from the bites of the ants. The songs they sing are remembering the battles of the past, how asiagpot'u haria (outsiders) killed their people, burning them alive. The reason for the biting ants is so the boys feel the pain their ancestors went through. Each new generation has bitterness and unforgiveness drilled into them through this ceremony.

So it was not really surprising we were treated in the way we were, but Euci and I still left Tuxaua Sapo feeling disappointed. There was no option but to leave with the pastor after three days. That night we slept in the boat. In the morning I woke up and started to pray. I felt God speak to me:

You are to stay with these people. Euci will go back, but you have to stay.

I told Euci what I had heard, and she said what I already knew: I couldn't stay because the chief wouldn't allow it.

So that morning I went back to talk to the chief to see if he would change his mind. Again he said no.

I talked to Pastor Jovito, and he was completely shocked by what I was suggesting.

"You can't stay here alone. They will kill you; they won't give you food. You cannot stay," he told me emphatically.

I didn't know what else to do. But as I prayed, I felt God say to ask the chief again. I did, but the answer was the same.

I wanted to be obedient, but it seemed impossible.

On the last day, when we were supposed to leave, I cried out to God. He told me to ask one last time. I slowly walked up the two hundred or more steps to the village, sure that the chief's answer would be the same. I was embarrassed and a little fearful to ask. As I neared his hut, I noticed that it was crowded with Indians. The chief was sick, and no one could talk with him.

"What am I going to do now?" I wondered desperately, knowing I had to speak to the chief.

I slowly edged my way to the front of the crowd and saw the chief lying in his hammock, a high fever raging.

Quickly I took my chance.

"I want to stay here for a few more days. Please let me," I pleaded.

This time, instead of an immediate no, the chief looked at me and said okay.

"Really?" I gasped. I thanked him and my heart leaped with joy. I ignored the angry looks from the other Indians who were cross that I had spoken to the chief, and ran back to tell Euci and Pastor Jovito.

"Are you crazy? You cannot stay," Jovito said.

But I knew God had told me to stay, and I knew He had made the chief agree, so I had a deep peace and confidence that was bigger than any fear. Daisy was staying too, with her sister, so I wouldn't be completely alone. However, my high spirits were quickly tested as I watched the boat with Euci and Jovito float off into the distance. I was now helpless in the middle of the jungle. If the Sateré-Mawé did try to attack me, I could only run into the jungle, which wouldn't be much better.

I walked back up to the village with my small bundle of belongings and went to ask the chief where I could hang my hammock.

"You cannot hang your hammock here. You cannot stay. No outsiders will ever stay here," he said angrily.

My heart sank.

"But you said it was okay. The others have gone. I have no way of leaving now," I replied.

He was very angry, but eventually when he realized I was stranded, he said something to another Indian who led me out of the hut.

At last, I thought. I didn't mind if I wasn't welcome in the chief's hut; any of the others would do. But the Indian led me through all the huts to the very edge of the jungle. There was a broken down, tiny old hut, dirty and full of scrawny chickens and sick dogs. It stank.

"This is where you stay," he said, and left.

I took a deep breath, knowing I would have to make it a bit more habitable before nightfall.

I got to work, shooing out the dogs and chickens. I was worried that the spindly beams wouldn't be strong enough to hold my hammock, but they seemed to hold. The walls and roof needed patching to protect me from the rain. I decided to go down to the river to collect water before making a little fire. When I was finished I wrote out Bible verses in my notebook, tore out the pages and stuck them around the walls to encourage me. I kept on expecting some Indians to come and see me, but no one came.

Eventually, exhausted, I collapsed in my hammock and fell into a deep sleep. The next morning I was woken by giggles and whispers of the village children, who were trying to peer through the thatch to see.

"Are you alive?" shouted the bravest boy.

"Yes, I am alive," I laughed, heaving myself out of the hammock. I looked around my new home. A mangy dog had tried to come back in the night. I shooed him away again. The floor was still covered with dung and feathers. I had tried to construct a makeshift broom out of sticks the day before, but I could see it would need some more work.

Staying with Kadete in Atuka, I had always been scared of jaguars. There were many in that area, and every village had stories of people being attacked and killed. Kadete used to laugh at me as I squealed in fear at the cry of a howler monkey, which sounded just like the growl of a jaguar. I had put the Bible verses up the night before to remind me of

God's protection. My biggest fear was of being attacked by a jaguar. But the children were not talking about wild beasts.

"Did you see the evil spirits? Did they come in the night?" another child shouted.

"No evil spirits came here. Jesus is with me," I said.

The children ran off to tell the adults, and I got ready for my day of visiting. I wanted to meet the tribe and talk to the women. So I set out early, going from hut to hut. But at each hut, as I arrived, the women became silent, and one by one they would leave. It happened at every hut; no one would talk to me. Despondent, I went back to my hammock. Suddenly a wave of loneliness hit me. I wept as I lay there, asking God for strength to carry on. I was also beginning to get very hungry. The villagers had not given me any food. Being from the city, I didn't know how to safely find food in the jungle by myself. Even locals can die if they get lost in the jungle; you need to be a skilled hunter to survive the journey. All I had was a bit of coffee, and that wasn't going to sustain me.

But I was saved by the children. Each morning they came to check that I was alive and then throughout the day snuck food to me: wild fruit from the jungle and ants. I once saw a little girl walking toward my hut with half a pineapple. Suddenly an adult shouted at her, and she dropped it, smashed it with a machete, and ran away. The adults were telling their children not to feed me.

As the days went by, I continued trying to talk to the tribe, but only the children would speak fleetingly before running away. I never saw Daisy. She was kept with her relatives, and I couldn't speak to her. Every day I cried; I felt so lonely and helpless. I read the Bible almost all the way through because I had so much time on my hands. Still, I would pray for the people and for a breakthrough. And then one day it came.

After nearly three weeks a woman approached my hut with some freshly baked manioc bread, still warm. She held it up to me in her hands like an offering. Hungrily I thanked her and took a bite of the delicious bread. I had been so hungry for so long that the bread felt like manna from heaven. Suddenly all the ladies from the village came with gifts of food. They had brought smoked alligator as well as pineapple and other fruits. Then they took me by the hand and we went from house to house. I held back tears of happiness. At last they were talking to me; for some reason I had been accepted.

I found out later that the chief had ordered that I stay in the hut where they bury rejected children alive, those with any kind of disability, not important enough to be buried in the cemetery. The Sateré-Mawé believed it was full of evil spirits that would kill me. There was a spiritual battle going on as I slept in that hut, over the bodies of rejected babies. I didn't realize it at the time, but later I would be the one to save children from a similar fate. I felt I had won the right to fight against infanticide in that place.

I didn't know why they hadn't been giving me food. Later Kadete told me it was just because they were mean. Each morning the villagers asked the children what had happened to me, and after nearly three weeks of the answer being "she is happy and healthy," they thought my God must be really powerful. They decided to treat me well, because if my God was so powerful, it could be dangerous for them to harm me.

I was much relieved, and instead of crying myself to sleep, I praised God for what He had done. A few days later I asked if there would be a boat to take me back to Atuka village to see Euci.

In the meantime there had been a harvest of *guaraná,* and I had been helping the women peel the fruit. The Sateré-Mawé discovered guaraná and made juice from it. I often wondered how the people could stay up all night singing and still be awake early the next day to work. I found out it was from drinking guaraná juice, which contains more caffeine than coffee. As I was peeling the fruit, someone called me to say a boat had arrived. I ran to find Daisy to see if she wanted to go home, and she did.

Quickly I grabbed my things and ran down to the river, saying goodbye to the villagers as I left.

"I will be back," I said as I waved goodbye.

The boat was a small canoe with two men in it. One spoke Sateré and Portuguese, which was unusual for an Indian. Daisy and I stepped into the boat and waved to the Indians on the riverbank as we slowly paddled down the river.

"I'll drop you near a small river downstream. There will be a boat passing in a few hours and they will pick you up," the Sateré Indian said in Portuguese. I don't know why, but for some reason he made me feel uneasy. The two men talked and laughed together the whole journey. I couldn't make out what they were saying. Suddenly Daisy started crying. She wouldn't tell me why, but I knew it was because of what the men were saying.

After a couple of hours they found the spot. The men were laughing as they dropped us off. It was about noon by this time, so we didn't think we'd have long to wait.

As they paddled away, suddenly Daisy clung to me and started crying again.

"What's wrong, sweetheart?" I asked, confused.

"I'm frightened," she whispered, her body shaking with fear.

I tried to calm her, but we were stranded in the middle of the jungle with no boat. I started to long for the security of the village.

Suddenly I heard men's voices. They were speaking in Portuguese. Then I saw them, about sixty men surrounding us, appearing from the thick jungle. They were dirty, many had no teeth, and they were looking at me hungrily as if they had never seen a woman before.

"God, please help us," I whispered as Daisy clung to me. I suddenly understood what had happened. The Sateré Indian had sold us to these men, and we were about to be gang-raped.

The men were drunk and started laughing as they saw us, saying we were worth the money and discussing who would rape me first and how they would do it. I was petrified. It seemed they were holding back for their leader to come, and then they would decide how it would happen.

When their leader came, he was dressed differently from the others, in army uniform, and was only a little older than me. When he saw me, he had the same wicked look in his eyes as the other men, and my heart sank. But then his facial expression changed completely—to an expression of deep concern about what could happen to me. He might have noticed that I was a city girl.

"What are you doing here? These men are going to kill you," he said.

"My name is Márcia. I'm from Rio; I am a missionary," I blurted out, my heart beating a hundred miles an hour.

"From Rio, really? Whereabouts?" he asked.

It turned out this man had studied on the same neighborhood street I lived on. Instead of releasing his men on me, he started talking about home. He said his name was Urbano and that he was a sergeant in the army. He was leading a group of laborers from riverbank villages to mark the borders of land that was to be given to the Sateré-Mawé. In 1978 the government had agreed to give the Sateré-Mawé the land to which it had moved the tribe. Urbano and his men were finishing the work.

We talked for hours; I told him about our work with the Sateré-Mawé, and he was very impressed. Eventually the men started preparing some food. A few had gone out hunting, so we had wild pig, rice, beans, and corn—a feast compared to my previous diet. It started to get dark, and no boat had come.

Urbano took my hammock and Daisy's hammock and tied them to the outside roots of a sapopema tree. He put mine closest to the tree so it acted like a wall on one side, then he put Daisy's hammock and then his own as protection. He shouted to his men, "This is where the missionary is sleeping, this is where the girl is sleeping, this is where I am sleeping, and this is my rifle. If I hear any noise, I will shoot. I won't wait to see what it is."

I felt he was an angel sent to protect us, but the next day the army sent a speedboat to pick him up. There was room for only one person, so we couldn't go with him. Urbano refused the boat.

"I will stay with you," he said.

I was so relieved. I knew what would have happened if he had gone, but he had given up his comforts to stay one more night, protecting us in the jungle. I was very touched and thanked God for His provision.

On the third day a boat arrived, not a moment too soon. We were taken to Maués, and I made my way to Pastor Jovito's house. To my joy and amazement, my leaders, Jim Stier and Gerson Ribeiro, were there with Euci. They had gone to Atuka to see us, but when they found I wasn't there, decided to go to Maués. I told them everything that had happened. Both Jim and Gerson gave me the comfort and support I needed. For the next few days they treated Euci, Daisy, and me like daughters, taking us out to eat and to the beach. It was a much-needed time of refreshing.

WHEN I RETURNED to Kadete and the Sateré-Mawé from my short break, I brought a team with me: Anabel Souza Lima, who was nineteen; Mara Helen, eighteen; and Luiza "Sateré" Brito, nineteen. I was twenty. Euci had gone back to Bible school, so the three of us set up house in the village of Atuka.

Mara was from a very poor riverbank community. Her father had paid for her DTS in manioc. When she arrived, she had a bad stutter, but as she learned the Sateré language, her stutter disappeared whenever she spoke in it. Luiza was later called Luiza "Sateré" because she became like one of the people; she looked like them and knew the language perfectly.

Kadete had built us our own home by this time, high on a hill overlooking the village and river below. He named the house *Salem*, meaning peace. *Atuka* means "a place where there is fighting," so Kadete hoped that the house he built for us would be a place of peace. It was not only our home, but also served as the school and church. We had started a school for the children and had arranged for food to be donated from churches in Maués, as the families were so poor that the children were often hungry and couldn't concentrate. Once a month we would travel upriver to collect the instant soup, milk, syrup, and guaraná. It wasn't much, and not particularly healthy, but as we doled out a bowl of food for each child, they would run out and jump into their canoes to take what they had been given to share with their families. The school food was sustaining the whole village.

My heart was still with the tribes that had not been reached, and the people of Monjuru. So after helping Mara and Luiza get the school started, Anabel and I went back to Monjuru.

We were based at Monjuru village for nearly three years, learning the language and trying to share the gospel. Unlike the people of Atuka, the Monjuru Indians were not at all open to what we were saying, but one woman heard and believed.

Her name was Zenaide. She was hated by the people because she lived with her son as if he were her husband. She wasn't a witch doctor—they are respected—but people recognized she had power to invoke spirits and put curses on people.

I could see she listened intently whenever I talked about Jesus, and one day she told us she wanted to repent of her sins and follow Jesus.

We gave her the New Testament in the Sateré-Mawé language, and she read it avidly. The change in her was amazing: she stopped living with her son and went out to tell the village what had happened to her. People listened to her because she was old.

Zenaide brought many of her fellow Sateré-Mawé Indians to know the Lord, but she wasn't content with just her own village. She traveled to other villages to let them know the good news. She even went to the Atuka village to preach there and learn from the other Christians.

Anabel became one of my best friends; we shared so much together as we cared for the Indians. They never built us a hut like Kadete had, but at least we were allowed to stay in the village instead of outside like lepers. Once a month, YWAMers would travel from Maués to see us, bring us mail and food, and support us.

When they came we would travel to another village called Kuruatuba. It took a day to get there in the YWAM boat, which had a small motor. There we would talk to the people about Jesus and try to encourage the Christians already living there.

After we had been in Monjuru for about a year, we started hearing about an isolated clan of Sateré-Mawé Indians called the Mokiu, hidden in the jungle. They hadn't been seen for eighty years and had "become like animals," according to the people of Monjuru. They had fought with some of the other clans and had fled to the area at the head of the Monjuru River. The "civilized" Sateré were very afraid of the Mokiu because whenever anyone got near them, the tribe viciously attacked outsiders.

Anabel and I prayed for them and felt we had to try and find them. Our problem was convincing a Sateré guide to show us the way. No one would go with us because they were afraid. But God was working, and He had spoken to a young Sateré Christian man named Chiquinho.

"God is telling me I must find the Mokiu and tell them about Him," he said bravely.

He knew it was dangerous, but he was willing to lay down his life for the clan.

So, praying hard, we left with Chiquinho as our guide, paddling for eleven days in a canoe. We then spent nine days walking through the jungle, making the trail as we went. Finally we arrived at the source of the river we had been paddling on. Dirt-colored water bubbled out of the ground. It was too full of mud to drink, so I broke off the stems of many vines and drained water from them into mugs. We drank thirstily.

With my body aching and head pounding from the long trek, I put my head in my hands. I was feeling dizzy, and the pain wasn't going away. Anabel looked at me with concern. "Are you okay, Márcia?" she asked, feeling my forehead.

I replied by vomiting into the bush next to me.

I felt feverish and recognized the symptoms of malaria, but I was in the middle of the jungle with no way of getting back but walking.

Chiquinho said we had taken a wrong turn and should head in the other direction to find the Indians, but I knew I wouldn't make it; we had to get back to Monjuru.

With all the strength I had in me, I started walking down the trail we had made to the river. It was easier not having to slash through the trees with our machetes but was still exhausting. I was drenched with sweat and could only concentrate on putting one foot in front of the other. When we got to the boat, I fell into it with relief. It was much quicker on the way back because we were paddling with the current. By the time I got to the village about five days later, I was seriously ill. They carried me to a hammock and I lay there exhausted. There had been a priest who had visited the tribe to teach them how to administer malaria tablets. They still had some medication with them. One of the Indians who had been trained by the priest gave me twelve quinine tablets.

"Because you are so bad, you have to take them all at once," he said.

Not knowing any better I complied with his instructions, swallowing each of the pills.

I tried to walk to another hut, but as I stood in the doorway, the world started spinning and I fainted. For three days I was in and out of consciousness. I should have died from the pills alone. The Indian had given me enough for seven days in one dose.

Every time I opened my eyes, I saw Anabel praying and crying over me. I could hear people saying I was going to die. At that point I was so weak I didn't care.

The Monjuru Indians were having an important cultural ritual at the time, with chiefs from many villages gathering together. No one was willing to leave the celebration to help me. At one point a Sateré man came to the village and saw the state I was in. He called all the chiefs together and rebuked them strongly.

"You must not let her die here. You have to help her," he said sternly.

He spoke with such authority that immediately a group of men loaded a boat with a few smoked monkeys (the food for the trip) and prepared it for the journey.

I had lost half my body weight and was only 38 kilos (84 pounds). The Sateré man who had championed my cause carried me down to the river, and Anabel took me in the boat to Maués. I later found out that that Indian was the same man who had sold Daisy and me to Portuguese laborers after leaving Monjuru the first time. He was evidently trying to make up for what he had done by saving my life.

I stayed in the hospital in Maués for two weeks. It was first time I had contracted malaria, and I was feeling depressed and sorry for myself. I was so weak that every time I tried to stand up or even sit up in bed, my heart would start racing. I couldn't stop crying. I felt completely broken. I looked like a riverbank girl, so thin, my skin all infected with insect bites.

On my left arm was what looked like a small boil, and it was really hurting. I told the doctor, but he said it was nothing. One of the cleaning ladies from the ward looked at it and recognized it as a fly bite. The fly lays eggs under the skin, and a worm grows inside your body. The cleaning lady was from the Amazon, so she knew about these things.

When the doctor came back, I asked him to check again. He was from Rio and wasn't familiar with jungle insects, but just to placate me, he cut open the infected bite.

"See, there is nothing there," he said, satisfied.

But my arm was still so sore; I knew the cleaning lady must be right.

She came to take a look, and put some rubbing alcohol on the spot. As she did, the head of the worm came up. She grabbed it with tweezers and pulled it out.

"Aggh," I cried, revolted by what I had just seen.

I cried into my pillow. This was the last straw.

"Where are You, Lord?" I cried out.

As I prayed, I felt God speak to my heart.

You are sick physically, but you don't have to be sick emotionally. It is your choice, He said.

I realized that even though my physical body was so ill, my soul and spirit were free. It was a revelation to me and I praised God, pulling myself out of self-pity and depression. This was such an important lesson for me to learn early on, as I got malaria many other times. But because of what God had told me, I didn't let myself wallow in self-pity any more.

After a month I began to feel stronger. I called my mother, and she arranged to bring me home to Rio.

By the time I landed back in the city of my birth I was feeling much better, but when my mother saw me she burst into tears. She said later that I looked like a homeless person—so thin, with my skin covered in sores, and my hair unhealthy and matted.

I convalesced at home for another month before making my way back to the Sateré-Mawé tribe in full health. Home-cooked food and rest had done wonders for me. My parents never tried to stop me from going back. They had taught us that we had to make our own decisions in life. They might not like those decisions, but they wouldn't stop us.

THERE WAS A FAMILY in Atuka that we knew very well. They had five children—two girls and three little boys. After I had known them awhile, the oldest daughter suddenly disappeared.

"Where has she gone?" I asked Domingas, the girl's mother.

Domingas was having a lot of trouble with her husband. He was getting drunk and fighting. He always seemed to be in debt. I knew her daughter's disappearance had something to do with him, but her replies were always vague. I never got a straight answer.

After living in Monjuru again for some time, I needed to travel back to Belém for a Cross-Cultural Training School. I decided to stop off in Atuka on the way for an hour or so to see some of the families. I stopped at Domingas's house first and then made my way to the others.

It was soon time for me to go, but suddenly Domingas called to me and beckoned me over. As I walked over, she pushed her youngest daughter, Aliete, toward me. Aliete was about seven years old; she was fresh from a bath, had on her best clothes, and was looking pretty.

"Please take her with you," Domingas said desperately, thrusting a bag with Aliete's birth certificate, hammock, and a few pieces of clothing into my hands.

"But I can't take her. I'm going to Belém for six months," I said.

"Take her. Don't bring her back until she is old," Domingas said, tears streaming down her face.

I found out Aliete's father had gotten into debt with the traders who sell sugar, alcohol, and salt to the Indians. As the Sateré-Mawé have no money, they pay with produce from the jungle, but they are always in debt. The last time this had happened, he had given his eldest daughter as payment. Indian girls work for the traders, cooking for them and cleaning their boats. They also have to sleep with the men. Domingas was desperate, not wanting the same fate to befall her youngest daughter. Her husband had allowed Domingas to give Aliete to me, as he knew he would be forced to sell her.

I had fifteen minutes to make a decision. I cried out to God for wisdom.

"Aliete, do you want to come with me?" I asked.

"Yes," she replied, smiling.

I asked if she would miss her mother—I was going to a big city and she might be afraid. She seemed to be sure, so I said okay, hugged Domingas as she wiped away her tears, and took Aliete on the boat with me.

When I got to the nearest city, Parintins, I went to see a judge and told him the whole situation. The fact that I had Aliete's birth certificate was highly in my favor. The judge gave me a "tutorship document," which meant I was Aliete's guardian.

With the document from the judge, I traveled to the YWAM base in Belém. When we came in through the front door, the first person I saw was Gerson Ribeiro. He took one look at me and one look at the little Indian girl, and his mouth dropped open.

"What have you done?" he gasped.

I told him the story and he understood, but we still had to decide what to do with Aliete. She needed to go to school and be in a family. The base was no place for her. A few days later I phoned my mom, telling her my dilemma.

"Bring her to me," she said simply.

I knew it was the right thing, but Aliete didn't speak any Portuguese. I decided to keep her with me in Belém for six months to teach her Portuguese, and then we headed for Rio de Janeiro.

My mother had come back to the Lord by this point. In 1980, while I was still in high school and my mother was forty years old, she had become pregnant with her fifth child. The pregnancy was very difficult and she almost lost the baby, but some Christian women came to pray with her, and God spoke to her clearly. He told her she would have a boy, and she should call him Daniel. She renewed her relationship with the Lord when she gave birth to my little brother. When I went to work with the Maxakalí Indians, she wanted to support me, but my dad didn't want to help or encourage my "crazy" decision. So my mother went looking for a job. Because she had had children so young, she didn't have qualifications, but ultimately she found a job as a school cook. She sent her entire salary to me.

Aliete stayed with my parents for six years. They treated her like a princess, and she loved my sister Maryangela, who was just a little older than she was. But then the time came for her to go back to her people. She was thirteen and if we left any later, she might not find a husband in her tribe.

"I want to go back and be a teacher," Aliete told me.

I said I would take her back, but in truth I was worried. In Rio she had had her own room and the comforts of a house; very different from the hut and hammock she would go back to. I hoped my fears would be unfounded and planned to take Aliete back to her people.

For the first month I took her to another Sateré-Mawé village so she could adjust to jungle living and relearn the language, and I could still give her the option of returning to Rio if she wanted to. Aliete had become part of the family, and my parents would have welcomed her back with open arms. But she was adamant about returning to the village.

Life was very different in the Amazon. Aliete vomited at the first meal of tinned meat. After a month we slowly made our way down to Atuka in the canoe, stopping off in villages along the way so she could meet and talk to the people.

When at last we arrived in Atuka, Domingas was the first to see her daughter. She came running to the water's edge, arms outstretched and tears streaming down her face. Her beloved daughter had returned.

Aliete gave out gifts to her family. They were things that she liked—pictures of movie stars and Barbie dolls. Nothing at all appropriate for an Indian village!

Eventually her father, Horácio, arrived.

"Why did you bring her back?" he asked without emotion.

He asked if she had finished her studies, if there was anything else for her to learn. I told him she hadn't finished high school but wanted to come home to her people.

"Well, send her back to finish," he said and walked away.

Aliete was in tears as she saw her father walk away, but she had made her decision. She wanted to stay.

After I took her back, I never heard from her and neither did my mother or Maryangela. One day in 2003 I happened to be in the area with my sister, and we went to find Aliete.

She was married with three daughters and was working as a teacher. When she saw us, she started shaking and crying deep, sobbing tears. We all hugged each other. We asked her why she hadn't been in contact, but she was too emotional to speak. Later her husband, who was also a teacher, told us that she had missed us all so much that she knew she had to cut all contact or she would want to go back. Life was hard in the tribe, but she had made the decision to stay. She had to do all she could to stick to the decision. My sister cried when she found out what Aliete had named her three daughters. The first was Maryangela, the second Maysangela, and the third Marysangela. Aliete now also has a little boy called Jonas, and she is studying for a university degree.

AFTER I HAD TAKEN Aliete to my mother, I worked with the Sateré-Mawé for another two years. In 1985 I felt my time with the tribe was coming to an end. Gerson said he thought my gift was in language study and therefore I should start with a new tribe and analyze their language. He told me about the Suruwahá. Two other talented YWAM linguists, Hulda Tavares and Bráulia Ribeiro, were already with the tribe, so I didn't think they needed me. As I prayed for the Suruwahá I felt a growing love for them, but I also felt it was not what God wanted. I decided to search for another unreached tribe, the Arimadi.

THREE

Searching for the Lost Tribe: The Arimadi

THERE ARE ABOUT one hundred and fifty tribes in the Amazon, approximately seventy of them with no outside contact. The Arimadi were one of these isolated tribes. They had not been seen for many years and were always moving, which made them even harder to locate. They would sneak into riverbank communities to steal food, then disappear. This was very unusual for Indians as they are normally self-sufficient, hunting and finding their own food. The survival of the tribe was likely threatened by some kind of internal problem—a fight between clans or an epidemic. I knew they were at risk. I also knew they were the people I wanted to help.

From 1986 to 1988, between working at the YWAM base in Belém and taking various linguistics courses, I took different teams into the jungle to search for the Arimadi. We prayed and cried out to God for them, but each trip came back fruitless. We could not find them.

In 1987 I was on one such trip, sharing water transportation with two other YWAM teams. Linguists Edson Suzuki (known as Suzuki),

Bráulia Ribeiro, and Hulda Tavares were with one of the teams, head-ing back to the Suruwahá with whom they worked. The other team was going to work with a riverbank community.

We had heard that the Arimadi had appeared close to a riverbank village a few years before. We decided to head there. First we took a Brazilian couple, Daniel and Fatima, to the Banawa tribe. They had recently finished their Cross-Cultural Training School and were going to the Banawa to try and learn their language. We were going to help them settle and show them how to start learning the language. So my team, along with Daniel and Fatima, left the bigger boat and got into a canoe to travel down a smaller river to the village. Suzuki and the other teams carried on up the river. They stopped a few days later at a small riverbank community that surrounded a lake in the river. Suzuki and the others got out to talk to the villagers and introduce themselves. They then sailed to the other side of the lake to sleep for the night in the boat.

But in the middle of the night they were awoken by voices. Peering out into the darkness, they could see canoes coming toward them. It seemed like the whole village was making a mass exodus toward Suzuki and the team. They were holding up kerosene lamps that illuminated insects flickering into the light from the darkness.

When the riverbank community arrived at the other side of the lake, they were wide-eyed, talking a mile a minute. From what they were saying, Suzuki made out that some Indians had arrived in the village in the middle of the night, and the villagers were very afraid of them. The villagers had come to tell the missionaries, thinking they might know what to do. But when Suzuki found out who the Indians were, he gave a gasp of shock. They were the Arimadi.

Quickly Suzuki, Hulda, and the others made their way over to the village. There they found ten very scared Indians—two women, two teenage boys, and six small children. The Arimadi were petrified of something, shaking and crying. Suzuki and Hulda couldn't understand a word they were saying. Indians always saw people outside the tribe as oppressors, but now they were so desperate they were begging for help, giving all they had to the missionaries, almost as a peace offering.

Hulda had compassion on them. Something terrible had obviously happened, but no one could understand what it was. Suzuki recorded them speaking, to see if later he could make out anything, but their language was completely different from any they knew. It was impossible.

Chico, the captain of the boat Suzuki and Hulda were on, traveled back down to where he had dropped us to tell us about the Arimadi. I was overjoyed. Especially since in one of our intercession times for the people, I had felt God say: *I will bring them to you but you must make them go back home.* I hadn't understood at the time, but now I saw that they were being brought to us. However, a day before Chico came, I had started getting sick with malaria again. This time it was cerebral malaria, which is much more serious. I was having fits and my body was going into spasms.

"We have to get you to a hospital," a team member said.

I was devastated. I had gotten so close, and now, when the Arimadi were here, I was too sick to see them. Chico took me and Bráulia to the hospital because she had also developed cerebral malaria, and the others went to the Arimadi. The team made a camp to be near the Indians and tried to understand what they were saying. They were with them for ten days. They tried to communicate and make them go back into the jungle, but they would not go. It was very dangerous for them to be alone in the village. Word had gotten out among the riverbank communities that there was a group of unprotected Indian women and children. The riverbank people found the Arimadi very attractive. They had pale skin and brown eyes. They didn't grow plantations but gathered whatever they could from the jungle, living under the shade of the trees. They were always moving and could not be seen from the air because their houses were hidden under the trees. Other Indians often called the Arimadi "primitive," whereas they themselves were "civilized" because they lived in huts and had plantations.

The Arimadi were also susceptible to disease from the riverbank people and from us. They had no built-up immunity, so even the flu could kill them. But every time the team tried to lead them back into the jungle they would scream and cry and hit the trees. We never knew what had scared them, but we guessed it might have been a war between families and they feared being killed if they returned.

After ten days another team member, Oscar, had become very ill with malaria as well. The others decided to leave the Indians in the care of the riverbank community and take Oscar to the hospital. They also told the national bureau for Indian affairs, called FUNAI, about the situation. FUNAI is the Brazilian governmental agency that establishes and carries out policies relating to indigenous peoples.

In their absence, Oziel, a riverbank man about eighty years old who had been looking after the little group of Arimadi, realized he could not afford to feed them anymore. He was very poor and didn't have enough to support his own family, let alone ten Indians. So he put them in a canoe and sent them downstream in the hope that they would find help elsewhere.

After a few days the rumors started coming that the Arimadi women had been raped and murdered. Oziel got in his canoe to see if he could find out what had happened. After a day paddling downstream, he saw vultures circling above the jungle on the bank of the river. He moored his canoe and went to search further in the jungle. He could hear a baby crying before he saw anything. Following the noise, he pushed passed the undergrowth and came to a small clearing. There, lying on the ground, were the two Arimadi women, dead. One of the baby boys was trying to breast-feed from his dead mother. Oziel held back tears as he dug graves for the women and put the children in his canoe, taking them back to the village. He gave the four surviving children to whoever would look after them and kept one baby, who looked about eighteen months old. Oziel called him Ari.

I arrived back a few days after Oziel had found the dead bodies. I wept tears of frustration, plagued with doubts that maybe if I had stayed I would have been able to help them. The story broke my heart. We were too late, and we hadn't been able to make the Indians go back to the relative safety of the jungle. It was one of the deepest traumas of my life. I was overjoyed to meet Ari, the Arimadi baby, but he was very sick and close to death. He was thin and weak and had infected insect bites all over his head.

"Will you take the child?" asked Oziel, watching me holding the little boy.

I happily accepted. Ari had beautiful brown eyes and a delightful bright smile. I felt privileged and overjoyed to be able to care for a Arimadi survivor. God made a way, and even though we didn't have much food, we were able to get to a riverbank village where there were goats, so Ari could have milk. For two months I looked after him and fell in love. Even though I was young and single, I planned to adopt Ari. He was getting stronger and stronger. One day, as I was down by the water's edge, I saw Oziel coming past in his boat.

"Oziel, come and see Ari. He is healthy and growing well," I shouted.

Oziel had come because he heard Ari was better, and he wanted to see for himself.

I proudly placed my healthy boy in Oziel's arms.

"He is wonderful. Can I take him for a ride in the boat?" he asked.

"Yes, of course," I replied, not for one minute thinking it would be the last time I would see Ari.

Oziel got in his boat and set off, never looking back. In a panic I suddenly realized he was taking Ari away. He had never said a word, just left with the child I had grown to love so much.

"Stop, stop!" I screamed, running along the riverbank, tears running down my cheeks. "Don't take him away."

Some of the children from the village joined me, and we ran and shouted, but it was no use. Oziel was getting farther and farther away.

After that I never heard from or saw Oziel again. He moved away with his whole family. I was brokenhearted and cried for days. I had failed again. I felt so much guilt about what had happened to the Arimadi. And now I had lost Ari as well.

I decided to go back to Manaus to FUNAI to tell them what had happened. I wanted to see if they would send someone to investigate and take the children back to their tribe, but nothing was ever done. Oscar was too sick to continue with the search, and our leader believed we needed to recover both emotionally and physically. So the search for the Arimadi was postponed, and I made my way back to Belém.

FOUR

Dead Branch, New Life: Edson's Story

AS MY LIFE was progressing, so was the life of Edson Suzuki, the man who would one day become my husband. We grew up in different areas of Brazil, but our lives crossed because of our hearts to reach the Amazon Indians. His story starts as a young boy living near São Paulo.

Running along the street to the Catholic church, Suzuki was headed for his First Communion class. At eight years old he would be celebrating with all his friends, and he didn't want to be late. The classes were given by a nun named Sister Maria-Elisa who taught the children prayers to recite and remember.

Like many Brazilians, Suzuki's parents were nominal Catholics and encouraged their five children to follow the traditions, even if they only attended church on feast days and holidays. His father, Yoshio, had come over from Japan as a small boy with his parents in 1937. When Yoshio was old enough, he got a job working on the farms in the countryside surrounding São Paulo.

Between 1908 and 1942 the Japanese and Brazilian governments made an agreement to achieve capitalist expansion and domestic tranquility. A program of migration, expansion, and international trade was implemented between the two countries, and many Japanese traveled to Brazil in search of jobs with the hope of becoming rich. Suzuki's grandparents were part of the exodus.

Yoshio was not religious, but happily adapted to the religious culture of his new home. When he was around twenty years old, his parents arranged for him to marry a cousin. But Yoshio had already met the woman he wanted to be his wife. Her name was Sumiko. She was also Japanese, but born in Brazil. When Yoshio asked Sumiko's father for her hand in marriage, her father said no. He offered her older unmarried sister first, saying that Sumiko could not marry until her sister married. Undaunted at flouting tradition for a second time, Yoshio simply took Sumiko to go and live with him and his parents when she was twenty-one and he was thirty. They were married in 1959, and one year later their first son Carlos was born. They had five sons in all. Edson was the third, born in July 1962.

The family moved to a city called Ribeirão Preto, close to São Paolo. For one year, when Suzuki was twelve, he got involved in the youth group at the Catholic church. They sang in a choir in the services; Suzuki loved to sing. At the same time, his cousin Sergio Suzuki became a Christian, and he talked to Suzuki about his faith. Sergio even took him to a couple of youth meetings. Suzuki was always open, interested in spiritual things. He appreciated the singing, but he never made a commitment to Christ.

Nevertheless, there was something that intrigued Suzuki about Christianity. He would even watch American preachers on television early in the mornings when the rest of his family was still asleep. He was always searching for the truth, and God was quietly planting seeds in him that would one day bear fruit.

In 1980 Suzuki went to the University of São Paulo in Rio Claro to study geology. In his second year, his roommate Edison's aunt invited him to a Baptist church service. He only went because he was invited; it was something to do. However, during the sermon he heard for the first time about the need to make a commitment, to ask Jesus into his life.

All this time he had thought he was a good person. He even felt he was better than the Baptists and was critical toward them, always finding fault. For six months he went to the services, but eventually he felt disillusioned and disappointed. He had expected Christians to be perfect, and when he realized they were just like him, with the same struggles, he felt there was no point in becoming a Christian. Many of the people he had met from church seemed to be hypocrites; they would say one thing and do another. There didn't seem to be any power or love in their lives, so he turned away from the church.

"I'm not coming with you to church anymore," Suzuki said to Edison.

Edison was disappointed, but he couldn't persuade Suzuki. He had had enough of church.

So instead of pursuing the religious life, Suzuki turned into a hippie and a rebel. He tried everything. Drugs, drink—you name it, he tried it. He dressed in an extraordinary fashion just because he wanted to be different and didn't want to conform. He would wear colorful socks, trousers, and bandannas, then team it up with an old-fashioned suit jacket of his father's. Suzuki was a mix of many different styles, and he loved that he couldn't be put in a box by the way he dressed.

Even though he had given up on the church, he was still searching. His life felt empty and he wanted to find answers.

One day Wilson, a friend of Suzuki's, lost a gold bracelet. It was very precious to him, and everyone helped him search for it.

"If I go to a spiritualist, she will find it. Will you come with me?" he asked Suzuki.

Suzuki was curious and agreed to go.

They went to the house of an old Brazilian woman. She gave them the creeps because she kept on muttering to herself.

"Who are you talking to?" Suzuki asked.

"It's the spirits; there are so many of them," she replied.

He shuddered, feeling uncomfortable.

The woman then said some incantations to help Wilson find his bracelet, but as she did, she came very close to Suzuki.

"You have this gift too; you need to develop it," she said.

As they left, Suzuki thought about what she said. He was searching for something and open to anything. If she said he could be a medium, he thought he might as well give it a try.

Over the next few weeks, Suzuki tried to develop the "gift" she said he had by himself. He would get a blank piece of paper and try to clear his mind to get the spirits to speak to him. But nothing happened, so after a while he gave up trying.

Suzuki was twenty-one by this time, in his third year of college. His grandmother was very interested in Chinese horoscopes. She told him she had done his horoscope and that this year would present two ways for him, a good way and a bad way. He would have a choice which way to take, but he needed to take the good way. Suzuki thanked his grandmother but thought little more about it.

It was not until he was a more mature Christian that he learned that consulting horoscopes was going to a counterfeit of the One who knows the beginning and the end. However, God used the words Suzuki's grandmother had told him to help him choose the right path.

His life was very busy. He had taken a job at a café on the weekends to fund his lifestyle of smoking and drinking. He joined the university choir as well.

Once a week, music students from other universities would come to rehearse with his choir. One week a girl from a Japanese background came to rehearse with them. Her name was Ruth Yazawa. Suzuki and some others from the choir went to eat with her, and she started to tell her story.

Ruth was a Christian. She was the first Japanese-background believer who captured Suzuki's attention. He'd met other Japanese-Brazilian Christians, but they hadn't intrigued him as Ruth did. She shared the gospel with him and his friends. He began to think about God again.

Suzuki was living with Edison and six other guys at this time. Edison would still frequently ask him to come to church, but Suzuki would always find an excuse to avoid it.

"I have to work. I can't come," he would say each time.

One Sunday after he finished his shift in the café, he was walking home with a friend.

A little while later Suzuki got home to find a group from the church singing outside his house. In Brazil it used to be common for a man to woo a girl he liked by taking a group of friends and serenading her outside her house. The church followed this tradition by going to the houses of new believers and singing worship songs to them. The group had arrived to woo Suzuki and his roommates to Christ.

As Suzuki walked into the building, his ears pricked up and he started listening to one of the songs. The words touched him and made him stop and think. The song was about God seeing life in a branch of a tree that looks dead. In a place where nobody expects anything good, God brings something beautiful.

A glimmer of hope fluttered in Suzuki's heart. He knew his life was empty, like a dead branch, but maybe, just maybe, God could do something with his life and make it beautiful.

By this time he had joined the others in the sitting room who were listening to the singers outside. Edison was next to him.

"Edison, I'll come with you to church next Sunday," Suzuki said matter-of-factly.

Edison nearly fell off his chair in surprise.

"Really?" he gasped with a big grin. "That is great news."

The next week Suzuki was ready to go. He took particular care with his clothes, wearing a huge, colorful belt from the Andes and an old army jacket of his brother's.

Another friend who wasn't a Christian came with them. The sermon that day was about not looking to others, who will never be perfect, but looking to Jesus, who is perfect. Suzuki felt the pastor was speaking straight to him. The reason he had left the church before was because of disappointment with Christians. The pastor was saying if he just looked to Jesus, He would never be disappointed. At the end the pastor asked if anyone wanted to give their life to Jesus. As he said those words, Suzuki's heart started beating faster. He knew Jesus was the answer, but he was struggling to surrender. Suzuki opened the hymn book next to him, trying to distract himself. It seemed that a sentence from a song leaped up at him:

"My friend, you have a choice today. Will you choose life or death?"

Suzuki could feel his heart thumping through his chest as he remembered what his grandmother had said about having two choices that year. He knew this was the good choice. He had to choose life.

"I don't know about you, but I have to go up," Suzuki said turning to the friend he had come with.

He followed a crowd of others up to the front of the church, and the pastor prayed for them. As he did, a peace came over Suzuki. His beating heart calmed down, and he knew he had done the right thing. Edison was overjoyed, and he and some others came to pray with Suzuki.

From that point on, Suzuki started to follow Jesus. Externally he had not changed; he was still wearing his colorful hippie clothes, but God was working on his heart. He joined a discipleship course at his church and was baptized a few months later. The pastor talked about having a choice in everything we do. Suzuki knew he had to give up smoking drugs and cigarettes. It wasn't a hard decision. He was so excited about his new life that he threw himself into it wholeheartedly.

About a year later the church was having seminars on spiritual warfare and the things that belong to the devil. Suzuki was convicted of all the New Age books and trinkets he had in his house. Before he gave his life to Jesus, he had wanted to experience everything. For example, he had bracelets stamped with the names of spirits that he wore for protection. This was not a cultural thing; it was just because he was searching, and his search had led him to the New Age. Suzuki knew God was telling him to get rid of it all, but he struggled to obey. He tried to reason in his mind that it was going too far to burn them, but then whenever he wore the bracelets, his peace would go and he would feel uneasy.

Okay, Lord, I will obey. Please bring back Your peace, Suzuki prayed.

He collected everything he had and took it all to the church, where they were having a huge bonfire to burn everything in the parking lot.

From then on he became more and more involved in the church. He had always been a person of extremes, and now he wanted to live as good a Christian life as he could. His language changed from using continual swear words to being punctuated with "Praise God!" and "Hallelujah!" Suzuki's old friends were not happy and complained that he no longer came out partying with them.

Suzuki's family didn't know about his transformation at first. He lived away from home and didn't see them often, but when he did go home and told them the news, they were not happy. They said he should stop being so radical in everything he did. He should find the middle road, be more balanced, and then he would be happy. He tried to disagree, to show them why he had changed, but it was futile. So when a little while later Suzuki told them he wanted to leave the university to go to seminary and become a pastor, their reaction was again unfavorable. His decision to be a pastor developed after he decided he wanted to give his all to Jesus. He wasn't happy to just be a Christian. He had read the book of Acts and it inspired him. He wanted to live like the early Christians and thought the only way to do that was by becoming a pastor.

"You must finish college, and then you can do what you want with your life," his parents insisted.

Reluctantly he decided to heed their advice, and with little enthusiasm went back for his final year. His heart was not in his geology studies. He sent letters to all the seminaries he knew of, asking for information about enrolling for the next year, but none of them wrote back. This was a little disappointing, but it didn't dampen his desire to pursue the career of a pastor.

When at last Suzuki graduated, he faced a big decision. The seminaries had not answered his letters, and he felt pressure from his family to get a job and help support them.

With a heavy heart he traveled to São Paulo to register as a geologist, an action required in order to obtain employment. It was February 1985. February is Carnival time in Brazil, and the streets are filled with people and color. The church always puts on a youth camp as an alternative to the Carnival, and Suzuki went along.

One of the preachers was Jim Stier from YWAM. He was talking about being a missionary, and as he spoke Suzuki felt something come alive in him. This was the first time he had heard anyone speak about missions, and he suddenly felt a deep sense of responsibility. Jesus commanded us to go, and Suzuki had to obey.

At the same time, he was looking for some kind of supernatural direction or confirmation. He wanted it made easy and clear.

At the church camp where Jim Stier was speaking there was another preacher from Americana, a neighboring city. The preacher had a gift of prophecy, so Suzuki hoped that God would speak to him through the preacher. The preacher prayed for Suzuki and his friends. He shared many prophecies, but not one of them was for Suzuki.

Suzuki's disappointment turned to hope when one of his friends extended an invitation. "Suzuki, would you like to come for a meal with the preacher from Americana?"

"Yes," Suzuki replied with a big grin on his face. He would be spending the evening with the preacher now. *Surely he will give me a prophecy there,* he thought.

Suzuki spent the evening eating and praying with the preacher and a group of believers, but again, no word came to him. Deeply disappointed, Suzuki made his way home. But then God spoke to him from Isaiah 30:21, "Whether you turn to the right or to the left, your ears will hear a voice behind you, saying, 'This is the way; walk in it.'"

Suzuki knew God was encouraging him to make a decision. God had already told Suzuki to go; he did not need another supernatural sign.

Suzuki decided to go and talk to Jim Stier about being a missionary.

"I want to go on missions. Can I join YWAM?" he asked when he next saw him.

Jim gave him a friendly smile and asked Suzuki more about himself. He then said that there was a course he could do with YWAM; the next one started in July. He was too late for the January course.

Suzuki knew if he didn't join the course right away, he would have to find a job and then it would be impossible to get away.

He asked Jim if there was any way he could join right away. After some back-and-forth, Jim agreed and said if Suzuki could get to Belo Horizonte by next Sunday, he would be able to join.

He couldn't wait to speak to his pastor. Excitedly Suzuki told him the news. His pastor had heard of Jim Stier and said that they would discuss Suzuki's case at the church meeting on Thursday. In the meeting they would decide whether they could support him or not.

Suzuki went to his parents on that Wednesday to tell them the news. They were furious.

"We paid for your education so you could go and do this?" his father said angrily.

Suzuki tried to explain, and eventually his parents relented and said it was his life, that he had to make his own decisions. But they wanted him to know they were not happy.

He hated to disappoint his parents but knew he had to follow this call. The next day Suzuki turned up at the church meeting. The pastor addressed him, saying that as a church they had supported people through seminary, but many of those people had never become pastors and had wasted the training. Because of this, they had decided to give him only half the support he needed for the YWAM training.

"If God is in you going, He will provide the other half," his pastor said.

Suzuki was happy with that. He went home via the bus station to buy a ticket to Belo Horizonte. Now he was going to have to tell his parents he was leaving soon.

He arrived home and went to find his parents. They were both in the kitchen. His mother was cooking and his father sitting at the table reading a newspaper.

"Here is my bus ticket. I am going on Saturday night to Belo Horizonte to do a missionary course until July," Suzuki blurted out.

Putting down the newspaper, his father gave him a long, hard look.

"We did not raise you to be a beggar on the street asking for money. This is no kind of life for an educated person like you," he said.

Suzuki told them he would not beg for money. God would provide. They laughed at his confidence, but after much discussion they let him go because he had made a commitment to the church. But he had to come back in July to get a proper job and have a "normal" life.

Relieved, Suzuki packed his things and set off for Belo Horizonte. God did provide the rest of his support through a generous woman who attended his church. When she heard of Suzuki's work and need, she wanted to help. Everything was falling into place.

Suzuki was in high spirits until he arrived at the YWAM base. The two-story building was in a rough area of the city, with unpaved roads stirring up dust. The base was like a construction site—no glass on the windows, no tile on the floor. The staff lived on the second floor, a little nicer than the first, where Suzuki slept on the ground with other students. As he was shown around by an ex–drug addict, his heart began to sink. Perhaps his parents were right. What had he gotten himself into?

FIVE

Go, Swift Messengers: The Suruwahá

DESPITE HIS SHOCK on arriving at the YWAM base, Suzuki's DTS proved to be a life-changing experience. It opened his eyes to the world of missions work. This was his calling, and now he prayed, waiting to hear from the Lord about the next step he should take.

"Have you heard? There is a woman from Belém here. She actually lives with the tribes in the Amazon," a friend from the base said to Suzuki.

"Really?" Suzuki was only half interested.

"Her name is Márcia dos Santos, and she is giving a talk on cross-cultural training this evening," his friend went on.

At this, Suzuki became curious. He had felt a pull toward serving as a missionary to Japan and thought about going there to live and work. Before that, though, he would need to learn all he could about cross-cultural missions.

Suzuki says he was inspired by my presentation that night. We were both twenty-two by now, but I had already spent several years with the

Indians. We didn't get a chance to speak at this time. I told the class about an upcoming Cross-Cultural Training School in Belém, and Suzuki knew that he wanted to do it. But he had a problem. His parents. They wanted him at home with a proper job.

Suzuki knew only a miracle would enable his parents to approve his plans to become a missionary. The DTS ended in July, and Suzuki made his way home. He prayed all the way for his parents' blessing. He didn't want to rebel against them. *Lord, if You want me to go to Belém and do the course, You will have to change my parents' hearts,* he prayed.

He was encouraged by Proverbs 21:1, "The king's heart is in the hand of the Lord; he directs it like a watercourse wherever he pleases."

Lord, if You can change the direction of a king's heart, please change the direction of my parents' hearts.

Suzuki walked into his parents' home, nervous about what he was going to tell them. He sat them down and gave them the news.

"Okay, it's your life, but don't expect any help from us," was all they said.

Suzuki was amazed. There had been no fight. His parents expressed their unhappiness but were not going to force their will upon him.

Suzuki was not expecting what came next. He was offered employment—an attractive geology job—that was exactly what his parents had been waiting for. It did not sway Suzuki; he was set on going to Belém.

Suzuki threw himself into learning all he could about cross-cultural relations when he arrived at the YWAM Belém base. His heart was set on serving the Japanese, and he even hoped to marry a girl of Japanese background. Relationship-wise, Suzuki had just split with his girlfriend back home in São Paulo. He had invited her to join him for the Belém course, but God had not confirmed this. They had agreed to end their relationship. Now, during the three-month course, Suzuki and I were becoming friends.

Near the end of the course, linguists Bráulia Ribeiro and Hulda Tavares asked Suzuki to join their work with a tribe in the Amazon called the Suruwahá. Bráulia was a Brazilian from a middle-class background, very radical and passionate, and years later became the national president of YWAM in Brazil. She and Hulda had been working with the tribe for two years, studying the language and recording words so they could translate the Bible into Suruwahá.

Suzuki's immediate response was no. He wanted to go to Japan, but he told Bráulia he would pray about it.

In our intercession time Suzuki asked God whether He wanted him to go to the Amazon. Expecting the answer to be no, he was surprised when he felt a "go" in his heart.

Just as he felt it, someone from the group spoke up saying, "I have a verse that I think is for someone, but it is not relevant to what we are praying about at all: 'Go, swift messengers . . .' from Isaiah 18:2."

When Suzuki heard the word "go," he knew God was speaking to him. He was to go to the Suruwahá.

Suzuki wanted to be obedient. He decided to go, but only for a year.

"I will only come for a year. After that I am going to Japan," he told Bráulia.

Suzuki went to his church in Rio Claro and told them of his plans. Now he was a full-time missionary—no longer a student. They offered to support him with a full, if small, salary.

That January Suzuki set out for what he hoped would be two solid months of jungle training with his team of four, including Bráulia, 24; Hulda, 29; and a man named Higino, 27. After that, the group would finally meet the Suruwahá tribe.

Arriving in Manaus, it was hard to believe they were so close to primitive indigenous tribes. Manaus is a large, bustling city of over a million inhabitants, wealthy from the money made exporting latex rubber from the *hevea* tree. The rubber boom was similar to the gold rush in America and made many Brazilians rich in the early nineteen hundreds.

Suzuki's group joined another team from the Cross-Cultural Training School who were also pursuing jungle training. They were supposed to travel to a city in the southern tip of the Amazon called Porto Velho for the training, but it was canceled at the last minute, and instead they stayed in Manaus helping in the churches. No jungle training in sight. At the end of their time they had made good relationships but were none the wiser about how to live in the jungle.

After two months they said goodbye to the other students and took the *São Matteus de Singapura* YWAM boat up the Amazon. The *São Matteus* helped riverbank communities up and down the Amazon and its tributaries, providing medical aid and sharing the gospel. It wasn't a big boat but could sleep about twenty people on hammocks. It took a month or more to get to the community of Delícia, which means "delight," a riverbank village where the *São Matteus* dropped the group off.

"Delight" was not an accurate description of the place. It was horrible, infested with swarms of tiny mosquitoes. To protect themselves the team had to cover up completely, not showing any skin. This was not comfortable as it was so hot and humid, and they were continually drenched with sweat. They couldn't carry huge supplies of water with them, so like the Indians they drank the river water. Sometimes they had purifying tablets to put in the water, but more often than not they just drank it as it was. Amazingly Suzuki never got sick from the water, but when he returned from the jungle, he would take precautionary medicine to rid him of any worms or parasites he might have picked up on the way.

Bráulia knew the people from Delícia and asked for their help in getting the team down the river a little way to the Suruwahá trail. They took them in their canoes, saying they had made a new trail and it was much quicker.

Suzuki relished paddling down the Amazon in the little dugout canoes. He looked around in wonder. The curve of the riverbank led into a beautiful bay with crystal clear water. There were manioc and banana plantations going up from the riverbank, which were farmed by the people of Delícia.

After a couple of hours the group reached the start of the new trail. They hoped they could get to the Suruwahá in a day. Close to the river, the jungle is very dense since the sunlight helps the vegetation flourish. The girls had small knives with them, and Higino and Suzuki had machetes to cut back trees or branches in the way. As they made their way into deeper forest, the trail became easier. The tall trees blocked out some of the light, so less vegetation could grow at ground level. They each carried their belongings on their backs. Suzuki had his hammock, a sheet, flashlight and batteries, one shirt, a toothbrush, and his pens and notebook for learning the language. Even though it wasn't much, he felt the strain as he walked through the hot jungle. They had also taken a gun with them to protect against wild animals like jaguars. They made sure to keep the gun out of the Suruwahá village; when they knew they were close, Suzuki wrapped it in a plastic bag and hid it under a huge tree that had fallen to the ground next to the trail.

Suzuki was excited and couldn't wait to meet the Suruwahá. However, although the team had been walking for nearly the whole day, it seemed that they still had much farther to go and it was getting dark.

"We will have to camp by the trail. We won't make it to the Suruwahá tonight," Bráulia said.

Suddenly the heavens opened, and it started to pour down rain. As they hadn't expected to camp, they had no tent or covering with them. They quickly fashioned a shelter out of large leaves and all huddled under it, waiting for dawn. None of them got any sleep that night, but it didn't dampen Suzuki's enthusiasm.

They set out the next day and at about lunchtime came into a clearing with a large longhouse hut, or *uda*. It was empty. The Suruwahá seemed to have disappeared. As they cautiously walked through the clearing, an old man with a machete came out of another large uda.

Bráulia started to talk with him, and as he spoke she began to look a little worried.

"What is he saying?" Suzuki said.

"Somebody has died," Bráulia said quickly, before asking the old man more questions. Bráulia didn't know much of the language, so it was hard for her to make out what he was saying.

As they continued walking past the uda, they found a big group of Suruwahá next to a man who had just committed suicide.

The group was grieving and crying. Silently the team backed away and waited for the Indians to come to them when they were ready.

The Suruwahá were very intimidating and aggressive when they first saw Suzuki and the group, but for some reason Suzuki was not affected by it. He didn't feel any sense of danger and just smiled, so happy to be with them at last. It helped that Bráulia also appeared relaxed and happy. She knew the Suruwahá and was not worried that they were pointing their bow and arrows, trying to scare them.

"It's all an act," she whispered.

Some of the men took the team's bags and starting inspecting everything they had. Suzuki and the others sat and watched, trying to explain what the different things were. Eventually the Suruwahá showed them where they could hang their hammocks in the uda. The Suruwahá were very amused at their hammocks made out of parachute material, so different from the Indian hammocks made out of rope from the bark of trees.

The Suruwahá are a very proud people; they hold their heads up high. For a long time Suzuki felt small and skinny next to them. It seemed that they were taller than him, but looking at photographs later on, he realized this wasn't true. He was taller than the Suruwahá. It was their attitude and confidence that made them more imposing. The Suruwahá are naked and painted red, but their nakedness didn't faze Suzuki because he was expecting it. Before he arrived at the clearing, he had taken off his T-shirt and was just wearing shorts, to become more, if not completely, like them.

The color red is very significant for the tribe, the color of dignity. The Suruwahá believe that when God created people, he tried to put red paint on them, but the paint did not stick, so he threw them away. They believe that the people God threw away became other people groups around the world. They say that God then created a man, painted him, and the red color looked perfect on him. This was the first Suruwahá. God was pleased and placed him right in the center of the world.

The red paint or *idahy* is seen as holy and powerful. The word *red* is even a term of endearment. Instead of saying "my darling," the Suruwahá say "my red."

In the following days the team started to write down the language using the International Phonetic Alphabet. Suzuki would try and talk with the young people and write down the sounds of the words.

Suicide was a constant topic because of what had just happened. There is a long, thin, poisonous bush root in the Amazon called *kunaha* that the Suruwahá use for fishing. But they also eat it if they want to commit suicide. It has a deadly poison that attacks the nervous system. Eventually the person cannot breathe and dies. At first Suzuki could never understand why the Suruwahá would kill themselves by eating kunaha, over such seemingly trivial things like a knife breaking or someone saying something bad about them. As he got to know them better, he realized the things that people attributed to suicide were not the real issue. There was often a deeper pain, but the Indians had no way of expressing it. The only way they knew was to fatally harm themselves.

It also became clear to Suzuki that the Suruwahá didn't like things that had been around for a long time. They keep their hair short for this very reason. They like disposable things. When they heard we in the cities build our houses out of cement bricks, they were astounded.

"That means it will be there forever. That is not good," one Indian said.

The Suruwahá children told Suzuki's team that they wanted to commit suicide when they grew up, to be with their ancestors. They didn't want to become old or sick.

Ironically, committing suicide is considered brave among Amazonian tribes. Ingesting venom is like trying to conquer death, showing that they are not afraid of it. When the Suruwahá die this way, they believe they leave the huge uda that houses the tribe and go to a big river in the sky where all their relatives who have committed suicide will be. People who eat kunaha are honored in the tribe.

Ten days with the Suruwahá cemented Suzuki's love for the people. Later, he was able to explain that Jesus was the only One who could conquer death. But for now, he would be returning to Belém for another linguistics course that he and I would both be attending. Suzuki and I would have more opportunities to get to know each other—steps directed by the Lord and intended for His glory.

PART TWO

Life Together

————— S I X

An Instant Connection

BACK IN BELÉM after my failed encounter with the
Arimadi, I looked forward to the month-long linguistics course held by
the Federal University of Pará. I felt so broken with disappointment,
but it didn't stop me from learning all that I could in devotion to helping other Indians. Suzuki was there, along with a student named Sibila
Hanzen. Suzuki and I seemed to have an instant connection. He made
me laugh with his jokes, and I was always happy when I was around
him. We enjoyed spending time talking and sharing our hopes and
dreams, but I didn't think that hope included us ever getting married.

The linguistics course was part of a master's degree for students
interested in analyzing tribal languages. We were not master's students
but wanted to continue our language study. However, there was a problem. The university wouldn't accept our applications. They said we
were not the type of students they wanted. We were upset, but there
was another option. We could take the course, but we would not be
given a certificate at the end, and the university would not provide

our accommodation and food, which it was doing for the other forty students.

It was so frustrating; we knew we were being persecuted for being missionaries. But we agreed to just attend the classes and forfeit the final certificate.

Gerson Ribeiro had arranged for us to stay with a pastor he knew. We moved into his home but never actually met the pastor, as we were studying and not home during the day. On the fifth morning the maid came to us and said we had to leave; she didn't explain why and seemed embarrassed to tell us. Without other options, we packed up our stuff and took it to the lectures. At lunch Sibila and I were in an anxious state.

"What are we going to do?" I said in a panic.

"Don't worry. We've got plenty of time to sort something out. Let's just study now and look for something after lectures," Suzuki said calmly.

Sure enough, everything worked out in the end. Gerson phoned at the last minute, saying he had found someone else to take us. This time everything went well; we stayed with an old woman who loved having us.

I had imagined that the course lectures would be really hard and we would learn a lot, but the opposite was true. We had already done basic linguistics courses and had lived with an indigenous tribe learning the language, so we knew more, in fact, than even some of the teachers. It was no surprise that the three of us were continually at the top of the class. We started helping the other students. They found out we were not allowed to receive our certificates and subsequently petitioned for our recognition. In the end we not only got the certificates, we were also honored as the best students.

Through this time, Suzuki and I were working together and sharing our lives, and I knew that I really did love him. My mother reminded me that when I was a little girl, I told anyone who would listen that when I grew up I wanted to marry a Japanese man. I have no idea where this thought came from. There was a large Japanese community in São Paulo, but we were in Rio de Janeiro, and I didn't know any Japanese people. Maybe I knew when I first met Suzuki that he was my Japanese man.

We used to spend hours talking. Sometimes our futures looked so similar and other times polar opposites. I knew I wanted to work with a tribe in the Amazon, and Suzuki wasn't sure.

When Suzuki and I had first met in early 1985 at the Cross-Cultural Training School in Belém, he had just broken up with a girlfriend back home in São Paulo. He told me that he realized he didn't love her when he met me. At the time, I expected him to say something more. But he never did. I didn't want to be the one to broach the subject about "us," so it had been left an untouched subject. It may have been untouched with us, but everyone else was happy to discuss it. People always used to comment that there was something between us and we would be good together. I thought there was something too, but nothing seemed to happen. When I was searching for the Arimadi, I had often taken boats with Suzuki's team since the Suruwahá were in the same area. We would talk late into the night while lying on the boat, looking up into the stars. It was so romantic, but still nothing happened.

Gerson always used to tease me.

"He loves you," he would say, smiling.

"I don't think so. He has never said anything," I would reply.

I found out from others in the linguistics course that there was a girl in our class who liked Suzuki. She was clever and looked like a model. I told Suzuki, but he didn't believe me. Then on the last day, I learned that this girl had a bet that she would sleep with Suzuki before the end of the course. I let him know, and again he didn't believe it could be true. That night she invited Suzuki to her apartment for dinner. We were supposed to go to the YWAM base together before I left for Rio. But Suzuki had said yes to having dinner with the girl, so I assumed I would have to go by myself.

I went back to where we were staying to gather my belongings. I was depressed because I wouldn't see Suzuki for a long time and annoyed that he had gone to eat with the girl. Suddenly he burst through the door.

"Márcia, come to dinner with us," he said, grinning.

"I'm not sure . . ." I replied, knowing the girl would not be happy if I turned up.

"Come on, I want you to. There will be sushi and Inca music; you'll love it," he persuaded.

"Okay," I said laughing, and we made our way over to where she was staying.

The three of us ate together, but Suzuki hardly paid the girl any attention, we were both chatting so much. Needless to say, she didn't win her bet.

We made our way back to the YWAM base that night. As we said goodbye, Suzuki gave me a card. In it was a Brazilian saying:

Distance is for love
As wind is for fire
It will extinguish if weak
But increase if it is strong

I read the words and looked up at him, trying to read his eyes, giving him an opportunity to say something. But he was silent.

Sadly I said goodbye again and went to my room. I decided then that I would just have to get over Suzuki; perhaps he thought our visions were too different, and we shouldn't be together.

I MADE MY WAY to Rio and spent nearly five months raising money to get to Australia to study linguistics further. It was very hard for me to raise the money, as the exchange rate was so bad. Each Sunday I would speak about the Indians at a different church, and an offering was taken up for me. But I worked out that if I went to a church every Sunday for the next year and they gave me an offering, it still wouldn't be enough for the tickets.

Lord, You promised You would provide, I prayed, remembering the lesson I had learned with the Maxakalí Indians. God does not forget His promises. I went to talk to Rev. Paulo Lockmann, the bishop of my region; I showed him pictures of the Sateré-Mawé and told him what we were doing. He was very touched and decided to send a message to all the Methodist churches in Rio and tell them to give the offering from the next Sunday to me. I was overwhelmed; it was exactly enough for me to travel to Australia and live there for a year.

I flew to Canberra and stayed at the YWAM base for three months to try and learn English before beginning the linguistics course at the

Wycliffe-affiliated South Pacific Summer Institute of Linguistics in Melbourne. I would be taking four courses back-to-back. It was going to be hard work.

The first letter I received in Australia was from Suzuki. I nearly fainted when I read it. He poured out his heart to me, saying he loved me, he missed me, and he wanted to be with me for the rest of his life. He said that he had tried to call me in Rio but didn't have the right number.

My hope that we would be together had died, and now here he was saying he loved me. I was so overwhelmed. I would lie in my bunk bed reading the letter over and over again. At the end of his letter, he asked me to reply to let him know if there was any hope. Immediately I wrote back saying I loved him too; I had always loved him. As I walked the letter to the mailbox, I couldn't contain the joy inside me and was grinning from ear to ear. I praised God that He would be so kind as to give me a future with a man like Suzuki.

Later I got a letter from Bráulia and her husband. They told me how much Suzuki liked me, as they always did, but they also told me of his experience with the Suruwahá, and how he had made the decision to give his life to this Amazonian tribe. My heart was at peace when I heard that, as I had always struggled with the fact that our visions seemed different.

Suzuki didn't receive the letter I sent him until six months later. He was alone with the Suruwahá for six months, not knowing what my response was. God used that time to make him sure of his desire to be with me, but it wasn't easy.

I now knew that I was going to be with Suzuki, but I had to wait a year to see him and finish the course. When I first arrived in Australia, I was told I couldn't do the course because my English wasn't good enough. I knew I didn't have time to wait another year until my English had improved. One day I found out that a family from the YWAM base in Canberra was driving to Melbourne. I decided to take a step of faith and go with the family. I would visit the linguistics school in person to try and persuade them to admit me.

My heart was beating fast as I walked up the steps of the South Pacific Institute of Linguistics. This was my last and only chance. I was taken to the director of admissions.

"Hello, my name is Márcia; I am here to see if you will let me in the course."

The woman looked at me kindly.

"Márcia, the course is very technical and difficult. You will be very frustrated if you don't even understand the English," she said.

This wasn't looking good.

Lord, help me, I prayed desperately.

Suddenly I had an idea.

"Give me a test. If I do well, you can accept me," I suggested.

She agreed and gave me a linguistics exam. By the grace of God I got full marks, and they had no choice but to let me in the course. By this time it was March, and the course had already started.

It was very hard at first; my English was so bad I couldn't even ask questions in class. We had to learn another language for the course, and I thought I would be allowed to use English as I was learning it—but that was the one language we couldn't use. Instead I had to learn Turkish, transcribe it phonetically, analyze the phonology, create a writing system, and write an ethnographic description of the culture, as well as present all my papers in Turkish. I would spend one day a week with a Turkish family to help me learn the language. The course started with forty students, but only seven graduated. I was the top student in my class. I had been so insecure about my English, but here I was coming through with flying colors. But it wasn't without a price; many evenings I worked all through the night, I was so desperate to learn.

God had another agenda for my time in Australia. He used it to heal my heart. I was so broken after my experience with the Arimadi, but God knew, and He showered His love on me. It started when I went to a meeting at YWAM Melbourne, where Loren Cunningham, the founder of YWAM, was speaking. He had heard of my story, but we had never met.

"There is a lady here who is like a daughter to me," he said. "You don't know me yet, but I know you. You work in the Amazon, and God wants you to know the blame for the death of the Indians is not on your shoulders. It is on the shoulders of the people who killed them. God is going to use you to help many other Indians in the Amazon. We want to honor you and bless you."

Something happened as he spoke. It was as if the Lord was speaking directly to me. Tears rolled down my cheeks as I felt a weight lift off me. That was the beginning of the healing. I felt so loved in Australia. The people at Wycliffe were very kind to me, and many YWAM leaders in Australia called to offer to pay for my course. I felt filled up and ready to go back to the Amazon, and back to Suzuki.

I flew home at the end of 1989, and Suzuki invited me down to São Paulo to meet his family. They were so warm and welcoming; I loved them instantly. Suzuki then came back to Rio to meet my parents. He and my father got on very well and would often joke together.

"Your daughter is so beautiful. Why did you put someone so beautiful on the earth?" Suzuki would say.

My dad laughed and agreed to give Suzuki my hand in marriage.

The wedding took place in July 1990. We had the ceremony in the garden of a beautiful house in Rio, surrounded by sixty of our closest friends and family. Our joy was complete.

SEVEN

Building the House

AFTER OUR TWO-WEEK HONEYMOON, we gathered all our belongings and moved to Porto Velho to join Bráulia and Reinaldo at the newly established YWAM base. Our first married mission together would be teaching a Cross-Cultural Training School. Soon we started talking about building a house near the Suruwahá tribe—a house that could serve as an even closer base. We didn't want to build in the village away from the Indians; we wanted to live with them! But the more we talked about a house, the more impossible it seemed. It would be very difficult to get the planks of wood, screens, stove, and other materials down the Amazon. It would also be expensive, and we had no money.

So we prayed, asking God to provide. We wanted to establish a more permanent ministry among the Suruwahá, and this house would mean we could stay there for longer periods of time.

We started praying with the other YWAMers at the Porto Velho base about the house. At that time there was an American/Australian family working there, Kent and Josephine Truehl and their three young daughters. They told us they had friends from the United States who wanted to come and help build houses. Their names were John and Denise Lundberg, and they were already in Manaus. John was a very good builder and wanted to donate his skills to a mission for a couple of months. They also had all the funds necessary to build the house. We were amazed and made our way to Manaus to meet the couple. We told them about the Suruwahá and our desire for a base nearer to the tribe so we could spend more time with them.

John and Denise were immediately excited by what we were telling them, but then we explained the difficulties. It would take a month and a half to travel by boat to the spot where we could build a house. We would then have to work quickly before the waters went down. If the water was too low, there would be no way to get out, and we would be stranded in the middle of the jungle for a year without food.

The jungle is a very dangerous and inhospitable place for everyone, even for the Indians. You need survival skills just to journey out into the jungle to find food. Once there, you need to know what is edible and what is not. And you need to know how to climb tall trees to collect food and to stay out of harm's way. I don't know how to make this clear to people who imagine that the jungle is like a theme park. It is not.

Despite the risks, John and Denise decided to go for it. Suzuki and I were amazed and praised God at His answer to our prayers. But as we encountered problem after problem, we knew there was a battle over getting this house built and establishing a permanent ministry.

We were a team of eleven and traveled on two boats with all the building supplies and food with us. Each night we would sleep on the boat. Three days into the trip, when the waters of the Amazon were very high, disaster struck. Our boats were moored next to each other, and the waves started pushing one boat into the other. At about three in the morning, everyone woke up as water started to pour into the second boat and it began to sink. The children were crying in the darkness as we tried to scoop the water out with any container we could lay our hands on. But it was impossible; we couldn't do it fast enough and the boat was going down. Quickly we tried to transfer all the materials and food we could onto the other boat, but sadly watched the sinking boat go lower and lower until it was completely submerged. It was heartbreaking to see the children crying as they watched their books and toys floating away downriver.

Our group huddled on the remaining boat, trying to get a bit of sleep until sunrise. Some of the food was lost, but we had saved most things, making the surviving boat very heavily laden.

"Shall we go back?" I asked, worried for the children. We could either all stay in the riverbank village until the boat was fixed, or separate, leaving some with the boat and the rest of us continuing on.

We all discussed it and prayed and felt three of the guys should stay with the boat until it was fixed, and everyone else should carry on because time was short. Suzuki and I were amazed at the courage of the team. They never complained and continued to be enthusiastic. We felt so humbled by them.

But the atmosphere was often very tense because of the high waters and potential dangers. At one point Josephine thought her youngest daughter had fallen overboard. She ran to the side of the boat screaming. We all jumped up, trying to find the little blonde child. After a few minutes someone realized she was curled up asleep in a corner of the boat. We all gave a sigh of relief but stayed alert.

We traveled on to another riverbank village called Caroço. As we arrived, the boat's engine spluttered and died. We were at the village for three days trying to fix it when a trader came past in his boat.

"Suzuki!" the trader shouted when he saw us.

The trader was Zena, a man Suzuki had made friends with years before on one of his many trips to the Suruwahá. We told Zena our dilemma and he was happy to help. The timing was miraculous. We transferred all the wood one more time onto his boat. Suzuki and I decided to go on with Zena and the wood, and the others would follow when the boat was fixed. We traveled for ten more days to the village of Delícia where Zena dropped us off. We now just had to wait for the others.

A week later everyone arrived. The boat that had sunk had been repaired and had picked up the others in Caroço, where the second boat was still broken down. The repaired boat got everyone to our meeting point safely, but the engine died the moment they arrived. We had a month to fix it and build the house before the water would be too low to return and we would run out of food.

There were so many insects that we had to work wearing long sleeves and with mosquito nets covering our faces. Even so, three of the team members got sick with malaria.

Josephine stayed with the girls on the boat, playing with them and giving them lessons. She had been a ballerina and was very delicate, but I was always impressed at how well she coped in the jungle. She never complained and took everything in her stride.

I would return from working on the house to find her on the shore of the river dancing with her girls, or cleaning the boat with classical music blaring out of the tape player. The girls wore long sleeve tops and mosquito net hats as protection from the insects, but again they never complained once.

When at last the house was finished, it was beautiful. It had three rooms and was surrounded by screens to keep insects out. And I was happy knowing that the wooden walls would protect us from the jaguars and other wild animals.

Kent had spent most of the time trying to fix the boat, and it seemed to be working. Our food supplies were low, but Josephine was very clever at bargaining with the riverbank people and traders who came past. She would exchange things we had for fresh fish to make our diet a little more interesting.

God was speaking to Suzuki and me the whole month we were there about establishing a ministry with the Suruwahá and His heart for the people. But we still felt the burden of responsibility for the people building the house. It was a dangerous operation.

After a month of hard labor, we waved goodbye to the team and the three little girls and waited for Bráulia and Reinaldo to arrive and travel with us to the Suruwahá village.

But instead of Bráulia and Reinaldo, another Brazilian couple came, Juarez and Lu Aguiar and their two children, two-year-old Liz and seven-month-old Caio. Bráulia had become pregnant with the couple's first child and so had stayed in Porto Velho to give birth.

After welcoming Juarez and Lu and getting them settled, we all made our way to the Suruwahá village. Suzuki knew where there was a trail, and we all set off early in the morning. But in the year since Suzuki had last been at the village, the grasses had grown, trees had sprouted, and everything looked different. We were in the jungle for five days trying to find the trail. It was often raining and was really hard on Lu and the two babies. Finally we decided to go back to the house, and Suzuki and Juarez would go off alone to find the trail. They took seven more days to find it. Lu and the babies and I were alone in the house, waiting for them to return.

The house was in the middle of nowhere, and we were terrified of getting attacked by jaguars. Only inside the house did we feel safe. Each morning we would poke our heads out the door, trying to listen for any sounds of danger. We then quickly ran down to the river to collect our water and scrambled back up to the house.

Despite our fears, we never saw a jaguar. Eventually the men came back and we were ready to go. But as we were packing up, Lu started to feel feverish. She had a flu and couldn't travel to the Suruwahá. If they caught the flu from her, it could kill them since they didn't have the antibodies to fight it. Suzuki and I decided to go on ahead alone to meet the tribe. We packed our stuff and put on all our protective clothing. Waving goodbye to the others, we started the two-day trek.

EIGHT

Under the Uda

HEAD LOW, watching where Suzuki stepped, I walked behind him through the jungle trail. It was tiring work; the jungle was steaming hot, and we were covered in clothing to protect our skin from insect bites. I had on long trousers and a shirt with long sleeves, as well as a bandanna around my neck and a scarf over my head.

While I was concentrating on avoiding insects and branches, Suzuki chatted away about the Suruwahá. He was so excited that I was at last going to meet the people he had lived with and loved for so long. He talked about the people, patiently trying to help me remember their names and how they were related to each other.

He explained how the entire Suruwahá tribe lives under one large thatched uda, surrounded by their plantations of manioc, banana, and sugar cane. Each family partitions off a section of the uda called a *kahu* where they hang their hammocks. Each kahu has a fire where the family cooks their food. There is a space at the center of the longhouse where people meet and talk.

The Suruwahá have been isolated in the middle of the Amazon jungle for hundreds of generations. Their first contact with the outside world was made through the riverbank communities along the Amazon. These communities feared the red-painted bodies of the Suruwahá, who would aim their bows and arrows or blowguns at any outsider in a menacing fashion. But despite their fearsome appearance, the Suruwahá are agricultural people, not cannibals. In 1978 a group of Catholic missionaries made contact with the tribe, and a year or so later a priest named Günter Kroemer traveled several times to visit them.

In 1983 FUNAI had made a trip to the Suruwahá. They took Indians from other tribes with them to act as guides through the jungle and to help with communication. It was through this trip that YWAM first heard about the Suruwahá. Their location and existence was confirmed by a missionary pilot who had flown over the area and seen the large Suruwahá longhouse. Since that time he had been praying for the people, that someone would go to them and tell them about Jesus. It was in 1984 that Bráulia first took a team to make contact with the Suruwahá.

Now, seven years later, around June of 1991, Suzuki and I were going back to the tribe, to live with them and love them and continue to communicate God's love in their language.

Before Suzuki had left the village after his first trip, he had told the Suruwahá he would come back with a wife, and she would have black skin. This was a step of faith in itself, as at that point Suzuki didn't know that my reply to his letter was yes.

Now we were nearly there. We took a moment's breather; it was sweltering with all the clothes on, but I preferred sweating than being eaten alive by the insects. Suddenly we heard a noise along the trail. In an instant we were surrounded by the Suruwahá, who seemingly appeared out of nowhere. My first impression was terror—all I saw were men painted red with bows and arrows directed straight at me. Some came close, the points of their arrows almost touching my face. They were yelling, but I had no idea what they were saying.

Suzuki did not seem to be worried at all. "It's my wife!" he said with a big grin, presenting me to them.

Immediately they started to inspect me. They couldn't tell if I was a man or a woman under all my clothes. I had hands grabbing me from every direction. The Suruwahá were so intrigued by me that they wanted to take my clothes off to inspect me more. As quickly as they tried to peel away my clothing, I put it back on. Suzuki was laughing, holding my hand. I felt overwhelmed but very grateful he was close by. The Suruwahá took my bag inquisitively and started going through my things.

All this time we were walking forward toward the village. Suddenly we were there. The trail ended in a clearing, and I saw the impressive uda in front of me. Women were sitting on logs around it, cutting corn and preparing manioc. Children were running around in and out of the uda.

The warriors were still trying to take my clothes off and I tried to fight, putting garments back on as soon as they were taken off, my eyes beseeching Suzuki to help, but he was enrapt in conversation with some of the men. The Suruwahá never wear clothes, and for them to understand someone they have to see them naked. I was so embarrassed and shy; I knew about the nakedness but hoped to break into it slowly. Now here I was, crouched on the jungle floor, trying to cover my completely naked body. Thankfully a woman came over to me wearing two *sukady* fringes that cover the bottom slightly, sort of like a tiny skirt. She gave me one and I put it on gratefully, somehow feeling a little less vulnerable.

This is terrible, I thought.

I wanted to make a good impression as Suzuki's wife, but I also wanted to run a million miles away from their staring eyes. I was angry they had taken all my things. The Suruwahá led us into the uda, and I tried to find where they had put my belongings.

They were laughing at me. They didn't understand why Suzuki had said his wife would be black, when my skin was the same chocolate color as theirs.

All I wanted at that point was to go to bed. I was exhausted from the trek, but I didn't know where my things were so couldn't get my hammock.

The villagers danced all night in celebration of our arrival. We were expected to dance with them. They danced in the center of the big round longhouse, arms linked over their shoulders. I could hardly lift my legs from tiredness, but they kept on feeding me bananas, which gave me extra energy. Eventually Suzuki was able to locate my hammock, and he set it up for me. I was so grateful, but as I went to lie down lots of children ran ahead of me and jumped in the hammock, their bright eyes shining as they giggled at their joke.

"Suzuki, please get those children out of my hammock," I whispered tensely. I was having a huge sense-of-humor failure.

"We can't say anything; their relatives will be upset. Let them be for the moment," Suzuki said, giving me an encouraging hug. I knew he was right, but all I wanted to do was sleep. My nice clean hammock was now covered in dirt from the children. It was just too much. I sat on a log, put my head in my hands, and cried.

After a while one of the little boys, called Tiuhawi, got off my hammock and came over to where I was sitting. He was laughing at me, but then he saw my tears. He walked forward and wrapped his little arms around me in a hug. I wept even more then, I was so touched. The Suruwahá do not hug; it is not in their culture. I felt the hug from this small five-year-old boy was an embrace from the Lord, telling me it would be okay. And it was. Finally the children left, and Suzuki and I were able to sleep.

Later I found out Tiuhawi had been born to a widow. As he had no father, he was beaten and rejected by the tribe. They would grab him and spit on him, or try to put tobacco up his nose to make him cry and vomit. I was touched that God had used a rejected child, one that I was giving my life to help, to bless me.

The next day I woke up and squinted to get my bearings. Everything looked different in the light of day, and I began to get excited about what my time with the Suruwahá would hold. But before I could get out of the hammock, I suddenly saw the chief, Hamy, walking toward the longhouse wearing all my clothes. My heart sank. As I looked around, I saw other men wearing different bits of my belongings. One man was laughing because he had my pants on his head. I closed my eyes in despair. The red paint from their bodies was now all over my clothes. I didn't think I wanted them back.

Slowly getting used to being naked, I spent my days trying to learn the language. I would go out to the plantations with the women and try helping them gather manioc. It wasn't easy. I could never tell if the manioc was ready or not. One of the first words I learned in Suruwahá was *danyzy*, meaning "stupid." The women would laugh and tell me I was stupid for not knowing things that were second nature to them. To the Suruwahá the jungle was the whole world, so they could not understand how someone would not know such basic things. Thankfully some of the younger girls took pity on me.

For the first few weeks, I was always comparing the Suruwahá to the Sateré-Mawé, who always came out better in my mind. The Suruwahá never shared their food with each other, whereas if a Sateré-Mawé Indian had a small fish, he would cut it into many pieces to give everyone a bite. A Suruwahá could be in a hammock next door to a family with very little food but never share their plenty.

I knew if I carried on with the comparison I would never learn to love the Suruwahá. I needed to ask God to give me a heart for these people.

My first week with Suzuki and the Suruwahá was a baptism of fire. Uhuzai, an eighteen-year-old boy, tried to commit suicide a few days after we arrived. If a person has no value among the Suruwahá or is not liked, when that person eats kunaha he or she is left to die. But if the person is much loved, then everyone does all they can to bring the person back. Uhuzai was of high value because he was a man and was also deeply loved. When his family saw he had sucked the juice of the poison root, they were desperate to save him. They had a half-hour window before it was too late. They put burning ash on his stomach and side to shock his body into taking a breath.

Suzuki and I watched what was happening, silently praying. The people had been trying to save him for hours. Finally they walked away. Despite their efforts, he was dead.

We were far away from where Uhuzai lay in his hammock and knew we couldn't go near him, but we could pray. When he stopped breathing, the family gave up. We were crying out to God.

Father, make him breathe, make him breathe, Suzuki prayed over and over again.

All of a sudden as we were watching him, Uhuzai gasped and started breathing again. Suzuki and I looked at each other in shock; God had just done a miracle. We ran over to his hammock and saw he was alive. Suzuki started calling out his name, telling him to live.

The next morning Uhuzai woke up very weak but alive. We later asked him what had happened. He said he had gone to a beautiful place by a big river, seen his dead relatives and wanted to be with them, but then he had heard Suzuki's voice calling him back and he woke up.

BEFORE I HAD JOINED SUZUKI, the people had decided he must be some kind of shaman because he would go into the jungle and sing loudly to Jesus. Singing is something very special to the Suruwahá.

"He is not a hunter, he is not strong, but he must have contact with spirits because he sings. He is an *inuwa*," they would say among themselves.

From then on, if a young man went out hunting and took too long to come home, his mother would often come to Suzuki to pray that her son would be safe.

"Close your eyes and see where my son is. Is he safe?" they would ask.

We believe that God gave us this opportunity as an open door to explain who He is and reveal His power. The people wouldn't believe in God if we just told them about Him. Suzuki had tried at different times.

"Suzuki, the things you talk about—when did they happen?" the Suruwahá men would ask.

Suzuki explained that Jesus died a long, long time ago.

"But Suzuki," they would reply, laughing. "We could show you a tree in the jungle today, and tomorrow you would forget it. How can you remember these stories from so long ago?"

We realized that the Suruwahá would never believe by being convinced in their minds. They had to experience the power and presence of the living God.

There were many dangers for us in the jungle. One day when Suzuki and I were walking along a trail, I wasn't looking where I was going and stumbled on a small bush close to the path. Suddenly I felt intense pain on the tip of my second toe on my right foot.

"Ow!" I cried out, looking to see what had bitten me.

As Suzuki inspected my toe, he saw the telltale sign—two bite marks with blood coming out. I had been bitten by a snake. By this time I could feel the pain traveling up my leg. Suzuki quickly grabbed a small stun gun out of his bag. It sounds like something from a movie, but we all had them, as they were very effective in stopping poison from traveling around the body. The tissue and cells of the flesh where the gun is pointed literally die from the electric shock. This hopefully stops the poison from reaching other parts of the body.

Suzuki was frantically giving shocks to my leg.

"Ahhh!" I screamed, begging him to stop.

"Márcia, this will save your life," he said firmly, not willing to give up.

Finally, after he had shocked me ten times, the pain stopped. I was able to walk home—much more carefully this time.

When we got to the tribe, I showed them the marks from the bite. They were all wide-eyed in horror, saying I could have been dead in hours. The Indians said that if they had been bitten by the same deadly snake, they would have cut off the leg immediately. This was the only way they knew to stop the poison traveling to the rest of the body and killing the victim.

After hearing that, and despite my complaining at the time, I became very grateful for the stun gun!

After a few weeks we went back to get Juarez, Lu, and the children. When I told Lu how the people had taken all my clothes off, she was horrified.

"Will they do that to me too?" she asked in shock.

"I think so," I said, laughing.

The next day as we made our way back to the village, the Suruwahá came out to meet us. When they saw the little fair-haired children, they were amazed. They immediately went to Lu and started to take her clothes off. But two-year-old Liz would have none of it.

"Don't you do that to my mommy. Give her clothes back," she said sternly in Portuguese.

The Suruwahá laughed at her bravery and started playing with the kids. They did not understand a word of what Liz was saying, but they figured out by the tone of her voice that she was rebuking them. They found it very funny that she was the only one who was not terrified by their presence. Undressing her mother was forgotten. We walked into the village, the Suruwahá laughing at Liz as she continued to make sure no one touched her mother. The family stayed with the Suruwahá for a year before starting a YWAM base in Boa Vista in the far north.

I began praying for real friends among the women. I needed their friendship as much as I wanted to offer mine. God answered my prayers, and I was able to bond with three women in particular—Huwi, Kuwa, and Kuni (Hamy's wife). Kuwa was a young girl who was in love with Uhuzai, the young man Suzuki had prayed would survive a suicide attempt. We would talk for hours about her feelings and her desire to be married to him. At the same time, Uhuzai was telling Suzuki he loved Kuwa. Among the Suruwahá, to initiate marriage, the woman takes her hammock and places it next to her new husband's hammock. If anyone disagrees with the match, they can remove the hammock and the couple will not be able to marry. This had happened to Kuwa and Uhuzai, and she was now deeply depressed that she could not marry the man she loved. She tried to commit suicide, but we found her in time and were able to bring her back. In the end Uhuzai married Bukari, Hamy's daughter, and Kuwa married Uhuzai's brother. Although she was loved by her husband, Kuwa never loved him as much as she did Uhuzai.

There was something different about Kuwa. She thought differently from other members of the tribe. Once when there was a flu epidemic in the village, we got a YWAM plane to fly over and drop off medication and food for the people. Most of the tribespeople were scared of the plane and pointed their bows and arrows toward it. Kuwa turned to me, so embarrassed by the reactions of her people. She was only fifteen at the time but seemed to be wise beyond her years.

"It is so hard for my people to understand. I know they are helping us," she said as the plane flew past.

I smiled, telling her she was right, they were trying to help. Kuwa was like me in many ways, clumsy and not very good at practical jobs. She couldn't make a clay pot very well, like me. I didn't feel so stupid when I was with her. We spent many happy hours talking together, working on the plantations, and cooking. Like my husband, I was excited that at last I was with these people, so far from the rest of the world and yet so loved by God.

NINE

Against the Current

WE TRAVELED TO AND FROM the Suruwahá village in an unstable wooden canoe powered by a 3.5-horsepower engine. We towed a smaller aluminum canoe behind us with our food and supplies. Although this enabled us to bring in more supplies than we could carry in our packs, our movement was still slow, and the trips were dangerous. Capsizing in the canoe was a very real threat during the rainy season, when the Amazon was flooded and the smaller rivers were choppy.

Suzuki had been writing to supporters for some time, explaining the problem with the boat and asking if anyone could help raise the money to buy a bigger canoe with a stronger engine. But his efforts were fruitless, and we had to make do with what we had. Having only one boat meant there was always a ministry gap of a couple of weeks. When one team left the tribe and a new team was going in, the new team had to wait for the canoe to arrive before they could take it back to the village again.

When I joined Suzuki I prayed and prayed for another boat, as our journeys were always fraught with danger. A trip that should take six hours took us three days.

During this time Suzuki and I decided to take graduate-level courses in linguistics. We had been thinking about it awhile, but the only universities that offered courses were in the south of Brazil, and we couldn't be away from the tribe for that long.

But then we found out that Unicamp, a university in São Paulo, was offering a master's degree course in Porto Velho. It was perfect for us as it was modular, with only one week of lectures every fifty days, so we would still be able to work with the Suruwahá.

We started the course in 1995. We left Moses and Lucilia Viana, a couple who had recently joined us, to minister to the tribe when we were gone.

One time Suzuki and I were preparing to go back to Porto Velho for lectures. We radioed some missionaries close by in the Deni tribe to say we were coming and would need to use their airstrip to get to Porto Velho. The journey to the Deni tribe should take us three days, but we told the missionaries we would leave very early in the morning and try to make it in two.

We piled everything into the canoes and I gave special attention to my notes. I didn't want them to get wet. We had forty pages of data from the Suruwahá language that we were taking back to the university to analyze.

Just as dawn was creeping over the sky, we set off. It was hard going from the beginning, as the water was very high and we were traveling against the current. Slowly we made progress. Previously, when the river flooded the banks, it had been possible to make shortcuts where the river curved. But this time when Suzuki tried, the waters surged against the boat, and we very nearly sank.

"I think it might be safer to stay on the main river," I said smiling, holding tightly to the sides of the canoe.

"I think you're right," Suzuki replied as he focused on the river ahead.

Late in the afternoon on the first day, it started to rain, softly at first, then becoming a downpour. I was sitting at the front of the canoe trying to shelter myself from the rain while Suzuki held on to the engine at the back, directing the canoe.

"Let's see if there is a place to stop," he shouted through the rain.

The sky was getting dark by this point, and the river was so flooded I couldn't see the riverbank. There was no dry land where we could stop.

We carried on, trying to stay as close to what we thought was the side of the river as possible. By this time it was pitch black. I had a flashlight that I was trying to use to light the way ahead, but all it seemed to illuminate were the giant raindrops right in front of me.

Suddenly we realized we weren't going against the current anymore. We were going downstream, and fast. In the dark and rain our boat must have turned around. It was impossible to get back upstream.

By this time the rain had turned into a raging storm, and I was sure we would capsize any minute. Then disaster struck. A second before we crashed into it, I saw a tree that had fallen into the river right in front of us. We were too close to avoid the huge trunk, and the current was pushing us toward it fast. I clutched onto my notes, screaming for Suzuki to do something.

The next thing I remember was that I was somehow on top of the tree, and Suzuki and the boat were nowhere to be seen.

"Suzuki!" I screamed, tears streaming down my cheeks along with the rain.

My hair was plastered to my face, and my clothes were as wet as if I had just been swimming in the river. I was petrified that Suzuki was dead and I was stranded in the middle of nowhere.

"Help me, Jesus," I cried.

After what seemed like ages, I heard Suzuki: "I'm down here! I'm holding the motor!" he shouted.

He had been under the water trying to save it, knowing that if we lost the motor there was no way we would get out of there. The canoe had been caught in the branches of the tree, but most of our things had floated away.

I was so relieved to hear Suzuki's voice. With a struggle he was able to heave the engine onto the tree. After a while the lightning started. I have never been happier to see lightning, as each bolt gave a second of illumination for us to appraise our situation.

Suzuki was able to get to the canoe and tie it closer to the tree trunk. We both crept into it and tried to cover ourselves from the lashing rain with some plastic sheeting. In the midst of it all, we both felt amazingly filled with peace and knew that God was with us and would protect us.

We huddled together—cold, tired, and hungry—waiting for morning to come. But we knew the sunrise would bring different challenges. The insects would come.

At daylight Suzuki started repairing the waterlogged engine. Our toolbox was at the bottom of the river, so all he had to work with was a spoon. I laughed that he was like MacGyver from the old television program—fixing the impossible. He was also fighting against the insects. There were hundreds of them, and there was nothing we could do without repellent or mosquito nets. Some of them left blood marks where they bit. Suzuki had blood pouring in streams down his face from the bites, but he kept on working.

The moment of grace was when I suddenly spied our thermos of coffee in the branches. I inched my way over to it and whisked it out. My heart beat faster as I checked to see if there was any coffee in it. When I opened the top, the delicious aroma revived our senses. It was still warm. Suzuki and I drank it as though it was nectar from heaven. It got us through the next few hours.

Eventually Suzuki was able to repair the motor, and we were on our way again. After a day we arrived at a riverbank community, and we stopped and got some food. In the final part of the journey, Suzuki had to rest the motor in his lap because the part of the boat to which it was normally attached had broken.

At last we arrived at the Deni village. The missionaries there had been so worried about us. The wife washed my feet and was so kind to us, getting hot water so we could have a bath. We both must have looked like drowned rats. The missionaries lived in a wooden house with screen windows. They had a stove, an aluminum bathtub, and even gas to heat the water. It was very basic, but to me it was completely luxurious compared to the way we had been living.

When friends and family heard about our near-death experience, it prompted a financial outpouring that helped us retire the old canoes. Two sturdy replacements were purchased, powered by not one, but two 25-horsepower engines. God continued to guide us and keep us safe on the river.

PART THREE

Stories from the Suruwahá

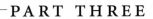

TEN

Blinded by Grief

A HEAVY, WET HEAT was rising in the Amazon clearing as Hamy, the Suruwahá chief, entertained us with stories of his great strength. Suzuki and I, along with our Brazilian team member Cléo and another missionary, Nivaldo, were passing the day with Hamy and his wife, Kuni. We were laughing until tears came to our eyes, watching him joke and flex his muscles. Petite Cléo was giggling on a log when suddenly Hamy lifted her into the air with one arm, a wide grin on his face. Cléo smiled with wonder as she rose off her seat, dangling from his arm.

Life with the Suruwahá was so rewarding. I truly loved them. We were not there to try to change them to be like mainstream evangelical Brazilians. We loved them the way they were. It gave us so much joy just to be there and be allowed into their lives. We simply wanted them to know that God loved them and sent His Son to die for them. We felt our relationship with the Suruwahá had never been so relaxed, so easy. It felt as if we were with family.

"Come to my manioc plantation with me," Hamy said after a little while. He was preparing to go and harvest some of the root vegetables. The Suruwahá plant manioc trees, banana trees, and sugar cane for food. Hamy, always generous with us, wanted to give us some of the harvest.

Suzuki and Kuni went with him, while Cléo, Nivaldo, and I stayed in the village. They walked through the trees until they came to the narrow jungle trail heading to Hamy's plantation. The Suruwahá never do anything in a hurry. On their way they waited and listened to birds calling high in the canopy above, or if they came across a fruit tree, they would stop and eat. The air, thick with humidity, sapped strength from Suzuki as he walked.

After an hour or so they arrived at the manioc plantation. The tall trees were almost fully grown, with thin trunks. The strong sunlight dappled through the manioc leaves, their shade forming dancing patterns of light on the dirt below. All was beautiful and peaceful. But suddenly Hamy started slashing at the plants with his machete, obviously upset for some reason. He had seemed happy only a few moments before, but now he was crying, his face contorted with anger and frustration. Suzuki was confused. He had no idea why Hamy had gotten so worked up.

"What's wrong?" he asked Kuni.

"He is hurting because our daughter Bukari died a year ago. She helped him plant these manioc trees. Now they are ready to harvest and she is gone," Kuni said sadly.

Bukari and her baby had died in childbirth because of complications. Their deaths had devastated her father.

After a while Hamy, exhausted, sank to the ground in grief, his anger spent. Suzuki's heart went out to him as he watched Hamy hang his head, totally deflated, a shadow of the person he had been just minutes before. Slowly Suzuki walked up to Hamy and put his arms around him. He didn't know what else to do. Suzuki was trying to show him he was with him in his grief.

Eventually Hamy rose to his feet and the three walked back to the longhouse, a much more subdued group.

When they arrived back at the uda, Suzuki told me what had happened. My heart went out to Hamy and his wife.

They left the manioc in the longhouse, and later I went with them to collect sugar cane. On the journey back Hamy and his wife started bickering. At first Suzuki and I thought they were joking, but we soon realized they were serious. We couldn't make out everything they were saying, but they were both very upset. Kuni had tears falling down her cheeks.

Silently Suzuki and I prayed for them. I hoped that their argument would be brief and soon forgotten. But things only got worse. Back at the longhouse, Hamy cut down his wife's hammock, which was just below his own, as is the custom for married couples, and moved it next to her mother's hammock.

By doing this he was showing he wanted to divorce his wife. Kuni, obviously upset, started smashing up the manioc and sugar cane they had brought from their plantation. When the Suruwahá are upset, they destroy their food and possessions as a way of expressing pain.

We didn't know how to intervene, but realizing Kuni and Hamy had no food to eat, we shared the boiled manioc we had with them. It was now late and getting dark; there was nothing else to do but prepare for sleep. As I lay in my hammock, I could feel the tension in the air. If something happened to Kuni and Hamy, it would affect the whole tribe. The other Indians in the longhouse had been as shocked by their chief's actions as we had. I looked over and saw Hamy lying in his hammock. He seemed to have calmed down; I breathed a sigh of relief and closed my eyes, waiting for sleep to come.

Sleeping peacefully, we had no idea that pandemonium was about to break out. A few hours later, with only the sounds of crackling embers burning and the sleeping tribe breathing heavily in the longhouse, Hamy slipped out and ran into the jungle.

He had collected the kunaha root for fishing, and he went into the jungle that night to find his stash and eat it.

It was pitch black when he returned after taking the poison, and he went to lie back down in his hammock, his body already reacting to the kunaha. Hamy's great-grandmother, Jasiiri, the oldest woman in the tribe, must have realized what had happened. She was so old she couldn't walk, but she crawled through the longhouse to Hamy's hammock. She woke me as she crawled under my hammock, and slowly I made sense of what was happening.

"Hamy, my child," she croaked over and over.

One by one, others started to wake up. They smelled the kunaha on Hamy and knew what he had done. People were screaming and running about, the men and women shaking their arrows and machetes in the air, crying out to the spirit of death not to take Hamy. It was mayhem. Hamy's relatives tried to make him vomit up the poison, but he was strong and wouldn't open his mouth.

Suzuki jumped out of his hammock and ran over to Hamy, who was lying rigid and shaking. Cléo, who was a nurse, gave him an antidote injection, but it was too late. He had taken too much poison; he had really wanted to die to escape his grief. Hamy was highly respected and loved. Members of the tribe had said to us before that if Hamy ever committed suicide, the rest of the tribe would kill themselves as well. We prayed this would never happen, but now Hamy was dying in front of us, and we were powerless to stop it.

Everyone was awake by this time. The village was full of crying and wailing. We knew people would be running to find poison for themselves to take as a reaction to Hamy's death, but in the darkness of the night we couldn't see them to stop them.

Among the Suruwahá after someone commits suicide, they start to chant death songs, which sound like the cries of mourning. But what they are actually doing is trying to blame each other for the death of their friend. The Suruwahá are especially vulnerable after a suicide; if they are blamed and provoked, they will often kill themselves as well.

Thankfully there were no kunaha plants near the village. Suzuki, Cléo, Nivaldo, and I started praying, crying out to God that more deaths wouldn't come from this. The atmosphere was oppressive.

I tried to hold Kuni, but she was completely out of control, screaming and flailing around with her machete.

"Hamy is dead," she wailed over and over again, shrugging off my comfort.

Suddenly Jadabu, a cousin of Hamy's, came running to me.

"I need your flashlight to stop people going to get the poison," he said.

"Of course, of course," I quickly replied, handing it to him.

But Jadabu had lied. He wasn't going to stop people; he wanted to find Hamy's poison for himself and eat it.

When he came back into the village and people realized what he had done, there was a fresh explosion of pain and grief. In the space of an hour, two leaders of the Suruwahá were dying. We knew this was really bad now. It felt like the last day of the tribe; it was that serious. We feared that they would all commit suicide and extinguish themselves.

Another Indian ran over to the longhouse we were in and handed Suzuki some poison.

"Quick, hide it so no one else can take it," he said.

I grabbed it and hid it in my bag, praying all the time.

There was no more poison now. The deaths would stop, for the moment. We kept on praying. The darkness was like a heavy presence over us as all, and the chilling noise of the Suruwahá singing their death songs echoed into the night.

Suzuki, Cléo, Nivaldo, and I had been sleeping in a kahu just next to the kahu of Jadabu and Hamy. We stayed in our kahu, waiting, watching, and praying.

Suddenly someone shouted at us to run. In the confusion we didn't see why, but then out of the darkness Jadabu's father, Aniumaru, came hobbling toward us with his bow and arrow pointed straight at me. He only had one foot, the other having been bitten by a snake and cut off at the knee. He walked with a stick and so couldn't get anywhere fast, but we knew he wanted to harm us.

"Quick, get away!" Suzuki shouted, and all four of us split in different directions.

Another Indian, Hamy's number two, a man called Kuakuai, saw what was happening and beckoned us over.

"Hide in my kahu; you will be okay," he said.

In the darkness we ran in, catching our breath. We had no idea what was going on. Aniumaru was shouting at us, but we couldn't make out what he was saying; he was so broken with grief at the death of Jadabu.

A little while later we saw Aniumaru coming toward us again with his bow and arrow ready to shoot. Kuakuai had left the kahu at this point, so he was not around to reason with Aniumaru.

"We can escape him because of his foot, but what if his son becomes angry as well? We won't be able to run from him," Suzuki said.

We all knew that the situation was dangerous; it would be safer if we hid in the jungle. Quickly we fled from the uda before Aniumaru got too close. With the help of a flashlight, we found a trail and followed it until we came to a clearing. We had nothing with us—I didn't even have shoes on—but we had to get out of the village fast. When we came to the clearing, about ten minutes from the village, we put some banana leaves on the ground and huddled together, crying out to the Lord for help and mercy on the people.

ONLY A FEW WEEKS before, we had welcomed a team of Polynesian Islanders called Island Breeze into the jungle. A YWAM group, Island Breeze is a Christian cultural arts and performance ministry devoted to rescuing cultures and sharing the gospel. The group that visited was made up of Samoans, Māoris, and Hawaiians. They had been touched by the Suruwahá story they heard from Bráulia, because in the past many Māori had committed suicide. Island Breeze wanted to come and do a traditional Māori haka (a spiritual posture dance native to New Zealand) and pray for the tribe.

Island Breeze performed among the tribe for three days and three nights, asking God for victory over the spirit of death in that place. At one time they did a haka depicting Jesus's death on a cross. It was a powerful time, and we felt God's presence with us. The Suruwahá were very impressed by the Māori men, who were so big and strong.

Before inviting Island Breeze, we had asked the Suruwahá permission for them to come. We showed them photographs depicting who the performers were. In the photos the Island Breeze team members were wearing traditional Māori costumes and holding spears.

"Yes, they can come. They are shamans—they are holding spears," Hamy had said.

In the past among the Suruwahá, a shaman always had a spear, so they assumed the Māori men were the same.

As Island Breeze worshiped God through the haka, the Suruwahá were transfixed. Suzuki and I translated all their questions. This was the first time we could explain publicly and in detail about Jesus and what He had done. The Suruwahá wanted to know what the Island Breeze dancers were doing as they performed the haka.

"They have been sent by Jesus to defeat the spirit of death," I said.

On the second night, Uhuzai, whose wife Bukari died, came with us into the jungle as we prayed before the performance. The Māori men were crying out to God on their knees for the Suruwahá, tears streaming down their cheeks. Uhuzai was amazed and asked them many questions about Jesus, the heavens, and the stars in the sky. He heard the gospel that night, and later, as we translated what the members of Island Breeze were saying in Suruwahá, he would repeat or echo our words, shouting so the whole longhouse would hear. This was a cultural thing—giving more weight to what was being said.

But now, only a few weeks later, the chief of the Suruwahá had committed suicide. We were devastated. Where was God? Hamy had been our hope for change in the Suruwahá. He had been so open and had huge influence, but now he was gone. We knew that Hamy had had an encounter with Jesus. The Suruwahá don't talk about spiritual things, which are too high and lofty. They must be sung. One day Hamy came to us and said he had been walking in the jungle and heard Jesus singing from the heavens. He decided to sing with Him, and he had walked for hours, singing a melody in tune with a song from heaven.

OUR LIVES WERE IN DANGER. We hid in the jungle that night of Hamy's suicide. The people would be looking for someone to blame; at that moment it seemed like Aniumaru wanted it to be us.

If that is what it takes, we are willing, Lord, but please stop the suicides, I prayed through my tears.

We heard crying and wailing from the village not far away. Everything seemed hopeless. We needed a miracle.

As the sky slowly brightened with the dawn, Nivaldo and Suzuki decided to go to the village to see what was happening. They left Cléo and me praying in the bushes.

Nivaldo and Suzuki, hearts beating fast, made their way through the undergrowth to the village. They didn't use the trail this time but kept hidden.

As they got to the village, they tried to see what was happening. As they made their way to the uda, a small boy of around eight years old recognized them.

"What are you doing?" the boy asked.

"We spent the night in the jungle. Somebody tried to kill us," Suzuki replied quietly.

The boy followed them back to where Cléo and I were hiding, but my friend Kuwa and a group of Suruwahá had gotten to us first. Thankfully, everyone had come in peace.

"Please come back with us. We are not angry anymore; you are not to blame," Kuwa said. A deep sadness had replaced the previous night's anger.

The four of us followed the group back to the village. When we arrived, Aniumaru came walking toward Suzuki. This time there was no bow and arrow in his hands. His shoulders were slumped in grief, his eyes swollen from crying. He could hardly speak, but he came and put his hands on Suzuki's shoulders. This is a sign of deep affection among the Suruwahá. Mourning is the only occasion when the Suruwahá hug.

"My son died," was all he said in a croaky whisper, his voice hoarse from crying all night.

Suzuki hugged him and cried with him, so sad for his loss. Later Aniumaru had no recollection of trying to kill us. Like Hamy, he had been so blinded by grief that he didn't know what he was doing.

Nivaldo felt he wanted to do something to show the Suruwahá we grieved with them. "I have my shotgun with me. When the Suruwahá are in pain they smash their things. I am going to show them my pain by breaking my gun," he said.

Silently he took out his shotgun and started to smash it. The Suruwahá crowded around, asking what he was doing. When we explained, they understood and were deeply touched.

"We are like children now. We have no one to show us what to do. Please be our *kahyzy*," the people asked Suzuki.

A kahyzy is a type of leader. Kuwa explained that it means "one who loves and shows how to love." The Suruwahá had planned on five people committing suicide to follow Hamy into the spirit world, but by the grace of God, the deaths didn't happen. The people had never experienced this before and didn't know what to say or how to act. It seemed that they were all ashamed that they were still there and hadn't committed suicide. They felt they had failed in some way and were hopeless and frustrated.

AFTER HAMY'S SUICIDE, the Suruwahá moved to a new uda. They then began a four-hour trek to bury his body. I couldn't go; I had no strength left. I just lay in my hammock in the uda feeling completely hopeless.

All I wanted to do was sleep and block out the tragedy. I couldn't even pray, but as I lay in the stillness, suddenly I saw a vision of heaven as through the eyes of the Suruwahá. It was filled with Suruwahá udas and a deep sense of joy and laughter. Angels, painted red with feathers in their ears, were singing in the Suruwahá language. The presence of Jesus was so strong. I then saw Jesus dying on the cross and diving into hell. The sound was so powerful the whole earth trembled. The Suruwahá see death as good, even desirable. They say when a person dies, his or her soul wanders the earth until there is a big storm. The sound of the thunder in the storm is the sound of the person leaving this earth and diving into the big river in heaven.

I had seen death up close that day, the power and finality of it. The vision gave me a new understanding of the power of what Jesus did when He died for our sins. I understood why Jesus had to die and felt the pain and the power of what He did.

I got up from my hammock and started walking to the burial site. For four hours I trekked through the jungle, crying all the way, overwhelmed at the revelation I had had, seeing what Jesus had done through the eyes of the Suruwahá. I had hope now that no matter how sad the situation was, God could still meet these precious people. Previously Suzuki and I had found it hard to explain the gospel to the Suruwahá. It never seemed to make sense in their context. But now I saw it through their eyes and I knew it made sense. It felt like I was having a second conversion—understanding Jesus from the Suruwahá mindset.

The feeling of the presence of God with me lasted for a week. I would cry every time I remembered the vision of heaven. In the midst of deep pain, God gave me hope. That hope was confirmed ten years later when we received revelation on God's providential work in the tribe. Suzuki and I were telling our story to a DTS group in Kona, Hawaii, in January 2009. The DTS was being led by some of the members of Island Breeze who had been with the Suruwahá. Suzuki was invited to speak, and as he did we realized what God had done through Island Breeze.

God had shown the Suruwahá a way beyond death. We were reminded that only a few months after Island Breeze came to the jungle, breakthroughs began and we were able to save children from infanticide. We were so disappointed with Hamy's suicide at the time that we didn't see the amazing work God was doing. He had broken the power of fear, suffering, and injustice that infanticide so darkly represented.

After Hamy and Jadabu, there were no more suicides for several years. This was the longest span of time ever remembered by the Suruwahá. (Another suicide reprieve has been occuring from 2007 to this writing in 2012.) We knew that what happened when Island Breeze came to the tribe was significant. It may not have looked the way we expected, but the tribe could have been wiped out. Thankfully they were still with us. We knew God was working. This was a new beginning for the Suruwahá and the start of God pouring out His Spirit on the tribe.

ELEVEN

The One Who Takes Your Heart

THE DEATH OF HAMY'S DAUGHTER in childbirth might have been preventable. We now realized the importance of helping Indians with health care, but there was a problem. Health care was available in the city. The Suruwahá had never been out of the jungle.

"We'll get eaten by white people if we leave," the tribe insisted when we talked about the option. No matter how much we told them we would protect them, they would not listen. We knew the biggest problem was not "white people"; it was the common cold. The Suruwahá could die from something as small as a cold because they didn't have antibodies to fight new illnesses.

In the end we decided that, despite everything, giving the Suruwahá a chance to have health care was the only way to help save lives in the future. We wanted them to see for themselves that it was safe, that they could trust medical resources coming from outside. We asked the leaders, and they chose Uhuzai to come with us. He was a deep thinker and would understand most everything he took in. With him we asked Ania, who always made people laugh and could ease anxiety with his humor.

In the end Suzuki thought it best if he stayed with the tribe, in case people got worried that Uhuzai and Ania weren't there and tried to commit suicide. We radioed the YWAM base in Porto Velho to ask them to send a plane to pick up three people.

We gave Uhuzai and Ania lots of vitamins to help their immune systems. We didn't know what they would think of the new world they would see, but they were completely confident and at ease.

I traveled alone with the Suruwahá to our house near the YWAM base in Porto Velho and tried to convince them to put some clothes on. Ania put his legs through some jeans, but tied the waistband around his thighs, rather than covering the essential part. He walked around the house very happy with himself. I tried to explain that they were meant to cover a little more of the body.

I drove them around the city, taking them to the hospital, the police station, explaining everything; they loved it and were in awe of the large buildings.

I thought it would be a good experience for them to see a supermarket. They were astounded at all the food. I tried to explain that they could take what they wanted and put it in the shopping cart. They didn't believe me.

We got to the fish section, and I told Uhuzai to take some.

"No, I can't do that. I have to ask the fisherman first," he said.

I attempted to explain, but it was futile. Eventually Uhuzai saw a supermarket worker, whom he thought was the fisherman, and he wouldn't take any fish until he had talked to him. Wearily, but with a smile, I agreed, translating everything.

"Hello, good morning, how are you?" began Uhuzai politely.

The supermarket worker looked from me as I translated to the Indian in front of him, not quite knowing what to say.

"Did you catch all this fish? It is very good fish. May I have some?" Uhuzai inquired.

"Yes," the confused worker said.

Happily, Uhuzai put the fish into the cart and moved on.

The Suruwahá were never shy or intimidated by the city. They took everything in with awe and wonder. At our evening worship services at the YWAM base, they would stand naked at the front, worshipping God with the rest of the group. Sometimes in the middle of songs they would try and take the guitar to play, or go to each person in the building, asking their name. It was exhausting for me, as I had to translate everything.

I hardly slept at all that week, both from the responsibility of looking after them and also because the Suruwahá would wake me up at any time of night and ask the most unusual questions.

"Remember that man we met? Who is his father?" or "Remember that dog we saw on the street? Why was it there? Can we take it back with us?"

Although the Suruwahá were very relaxed, they kept their bows and arrows by the door, just in case. Different people asked to buy them throughout the week, but Uhuzai and Ania never agreed, in case they needed them for protection. On the last day they happily gave their bows and arrows away, as they felt safe now that they were going home.

When we got back to the tribe, we were curious as to how Uhuzai and Ania would describe their experiences. They talked about the people and the houses the most, and, of course, the supermarkets.

After Hamy died, Kuakuai had become chief. He had six sons and a little girl and was considered very blessed by the Suruwahá. His wife then went on to have another boy, but when he was born his umbilical cord got infected and he became very sick. We were in Porto Velho at the time, so Moses and Lucilia brought the couple to us with the little boy. We took him to the hospital, and the doctors found he had blood poisoning. It was touch and go for a long time. Thankfully after treatment he got better, but he would have died in the jungle.

Kuakuai was very proud of his wife and didn't want other men looking at her. They were both naked in their little hospital room, but when the doctors came in, Kuakuai would lay his wife on the bed and cover her body and head with a blanket. Suzuki and I tried to explain it would help if they put clothes on, but we couldn't convince them. We were just pleased because lives were being saved now that the Suruwahá were no longer afraid to come out of the jungle.

One day, back with the tribe, Aniumaru—then age about fifty—beckoned me over.

"Do you know the names of Jesus?" he asked.

"What do you mean?" I asked, confused.

"Get a pen and paper and I will tell you."

Quickly I grabbed Suzuki, and with my pen and paper we went to sit by Aniumaru's hammock.

"The first name is *Hanadawa*," he said, and then went into a description of the name. Hanadawa means "the one who calls you." But it isn't just any call. Aniumaru described it as a call the Suruwahá give when they think someone is lost in the jungle. The call gives the lost person peace, lets them know they are not alone.

I started weeping because I knew from experience what this meant. A couple of nights before, all the men had gone on a hunting trip; only the women and children, Suzuki and I, and a very old man were left in the longhouse for a few days. At night the women were very afraid. They were so scared that on the first night they stayed up all night singing, to make a noise that would scare any evil spirits from coming near them. The second night was the same. Suzuki and I stayed up with them, but by the third night we were too exhausted. We prayed that God would give them peace and then fell asleep. At about 2:00 a.m. one of the women came running to our hammocks.

"Listen, Jesus is shouting to us," she said with wide eyes.

"What do you mean?" I replied groggily. I couldn't hear anything.

"Yes, He is calling. Can't you hear?" she went on.

I tried to listen but couldn't hear what she was talking about, so I went back to sleep. The women had stopped singing and were sleeping now too.

In the morning I asked what had happened. They said they had been very scared, but then they heard Jesus call to tell them they were not alone, and their hearts became peaceful and they could sleep. Jesus had already shown himself to be Hanadawa to the Suruwahá.

Aniumaru continued. "The next name is *Mitadawa*." This means "the one who paid a price to gain something." Death is also involved, as the thing paid is dead, such as an animal or produce.

"God paid a very expensive price to have us," said Aniumaru.

The third name is *Agadawa*. Agadawa is "the one who takes your heart."

"When we die, our heart is desperate, wandering the horizon, but He takes the heart home," explained Aniumaru. Suzuki and I looked at each other in amazement as we wrote down the new words, staggered at the characteristics of Jesus that Aniumaru was describing.

The final word is *Agijawadawa*—"the one who frees you so you can follow him." Aniumaru described it as someone who frees a dog that is tied up.

"How do you know these names?" Suzuki asked.

"He told me," Aniumaru said, shrugging as if it was the most natural thing in the world. The names had come as he was singing to Jesus.

TWELVE

Jasiuwa Bahi

AS THE SURUWAHÁ were having experiences of God and becoming followers of Jesus, we didn't know what to call them. To name them "believers" was too cognitive because *believe* involves a thought process, and what they were experiencing was much deeper. We also didn't want them to put them in a box, separating them from the other Suruwahá. Suzuki and I talked about it a lot.

One of the many Suruwahá to be transformed was Asia, the shaman. His daughter had committed suicide, and Asia, devastated, had decided to do the same. But as he ran through the jungle to find the poison root, Jesus appeared in front of him.

Jesus told Asia not to follow his daughter but go back to the tribe and live. Asia ran back to his people and immediately came to find us.

"I saw Jesus. He told me not to commit suicide!" Asia said excitedly.

Suzuki and I looked at each other in surprise; it was the last thing we were expecting to hear.

"What did he look like? Suzuki asked.

"Like us—he was naked and painted red, but he was big and strong!"

"How did you know it was Jesus?" Suzuki said, amazed.

"I know many spirits, but I knew this was Jesus because He was different. His eyes were shining like fire, and when he spoke His voice was so powerful, but it was also gentle," Asia said.

We were excited but still not a hundred percent certain of what happened. I felt if it really was Jesus, Asia would change. You cannot meet with the living God and stay the same. And over the next few days and weeks, he did.

Later in the week another shaman from the village had gone out in his canoe with his family and all their belongings. The river was high, and they were hit by a falling tree. Even though they were able to save themselves, they lost everything else. Their machete, hammocks, and supplies were all gone. Devastated, the shaman returned to the tribe with his family. Among the Suruwahá a person's hammock is a prized possession—it takes months to make—and the men's hammocks are particularly impressive, much larger than the women's. Losing a hammock is like losing a house. So when the shaman and his family returned, everyone was very tense.

"He will commit suicide," they whispered to each other as they watched him sitting on a log. His wife and daughters had left the uda, they were so scared and nervous about what he would do. But by morning he was still on the log; he hadn't committed suicide. Asia, who was not from the same family as this man or a close friend, went to every family in the tribe asking for a thread from their hammocks. The initiative and humility of this act was dramatic. The Suruwahá never ask for things from each other, but Asia humbled himself for the sake of the one in need. After collecting all the threads, he had enough for the wife to weave a new hammock for her husband, which she could do in a day as the threads were already prepared, thus saving him from committing suicide. When people talked about what Asia had done, they said in amazement that something had happened to his heart.

Asia's heart also reached out to the needy. At that time we prayed for a young Indian to catch a tapir. He had never caught one before, but after we prayed he caught three in one day, which was unheard of in the tribe. Everyone was very excited, and it became almost a fashion to ask

Jesus for whatever they wanted. One day Suzuki and I were lying in our hammocks talking with Asia. Another young Indian walked past and asked us to pray to Jesus for him.

"I am going hunting. Please pray Jesus will help me kill a tapir," he said.

"We'll pray!" Suzuki said, smiling.

But then suddenly I saw Asia's face. He looked frustrated, angry even.

"What is it?" I asked.

"Jesus is not going to give us anything," he said with passion.

Suzuki and I looked at each other.

"Why not?" I asked.

"He will say to us *haba* (which means turning your face away as you say no) because he sees how we treat our widows and orphans, and He will not be pleased," he said.

Asia meant what he said. We were amazed to see how he started to take care of the widows and orphans, something a person with the standing of a witch doctor would never do.

At one time a little orphan girl, about four years old, fell into a hole and got trapped. Almost everyone in the tribe considered her worthless; they just laughed at her screams of fear. Suzuki and I tried to get her out, but she was caught, and in her terror was making it hard for us to help her. Suddenly Asia went over to her and started speaking gently to calm her. When she stopped crying, he was able to ease her out and save her life. The other Suruwahá were dumbstruck. They had no words to explain the change in Asia.

Shamans often went into the jungle at night and sang to get possessed by spirits. Then they came back to the tribe and passed on the song. One day when Suzuki and I returned after two weeks away from the tribe, we had heard Asia had gone into the jungle just outside the uda to sing. He had sung the most beautiful song, and the whole tribe had been so touched they were still talking about it.

Suzuki and I felt deflated. We were sure Asia knew Jesus, but from what it sounded like, he was still being possessed by spirits.

"What were you singing?" we asked when we saw him.

"I was not singing," he replied, walking away.

He would not tell us, but later, when we heard descriptions of his song, I was taken aback. He was singing about an angel walking along a trail in heaven beside a plantation of cashew fruit. The cashew fruit represents the heart; it has the same shape and the same color. The red of the fruit was standing out brightly against the green of the leaves. As the angel walked away, he saw a log on the trail. On it were cashew nuts, but without the fruit to which they were normally attached.

"Who ate the fruit?" the angel asked.

"It must have been Jesus," Asia said. "Jesus ate the fruit and made my heart sweet."

The song was so symbolic, explaining perfectly how Jesus is our atonement, taking away our sin. It described the transformation of our hearts when we let Jesus in, and explained it infinitely better than Suzuki or I could have done.

ARAGUNASIHINI was a Suruwahá man in his twenties. He was married to Harakady and they had two daughters. To have no sons was very bad luck. If they had another girl, the baby would have to be abandoned in the jungle. When Harakady became pregnant for the third time, she and her husband were both very nervous. We all knew what would happen if it was a girl. Sure enough, Harakady gave birth to another little girl, Tabaru, which means "released."

Harakady had told me that she was terrified she might have another girl. I told her many times that I would be there to help her if she needed it. The day of her delivery, she walked through my kahu, her eyes crying for help. I knew what those eyes were saying, so I followed her into the jungle. A little while later she gave birth to a beautiful girl. When I told her she had had another girl she started crying and left the baby in the bushes. Alone with the infant, I decided to cut the cord and bring the baby back to the uda. I placed her in Harakady's hammock. For two days she would not touch the baby, scared of what the others in the tribe would say. But on the third day she couldn't take it anymore. She picked up her baby and started to care for her.

After a few days the family bonded with Tabaru and loved her as much as their other daughters. A few years later Aragunasihini thanked me for saving his daughter.

"She is the most beautiful of all my children, and she is with us because of you. Thank you," he said solemnly.

A little while later Harakady became pregnant with their fourth child. She was tense and nervous throughout the whole pregnancy. If they had another girl, both parents would have to commit suicide; it was what was expected. I prayed every day that they might have a boy, and sent out letters to everyone I knew, begging them to pray. I couldn't bear to lose this wonderful couple.

Harakady went into labor, and there was much rejoicing when she gave birth to a healthy boy. They named him Jasiwakazuhawydary, which means "Jesus ordained him."

HUDURU, although only thirty, was a widow. She was a good friend of mine and we spent many hours together. As time went by, Huduru seemed to lose her joy. From what I could make out, she had become jealous of her fifteen-year-old daughter, who was very beautiful and was getting a lot of attention from the men. Huduru, on the other hand, although still young and one of the most beautiful women in the tribe, was discarded.

This root of bitterness took over her life, and she became very angry. One day she found out her daughter had slept with someone. She was so angry she ate the poison root. Huduru lay dying in her hammock, but no one came to help her. They blamed her for her husband's suicide and left her to die. Suzuki and I ran to her side, trying to make her vomit up the poison, but we were too late. I held her in my arms as she died. Suzuki and I were both crying for her; her death was such a waste.

The next morning Aniumaru came to us. He had been watching everything from his hammock.

"I had the most beautiful experience last night," he said.

"What happened?" I asked, wondering what could have been so beautiful when Huduru died.

"I talked to Jesus. My heart went to His heart in heaven, and I asked him to take Huduru's heart. Jesus looked sad and said He couldn't do anything. She had wanted to die and her heart was full of anger," he said.

Aniumaru said he had been disappointed with Jesus, for he was sure Jesus could have answered his prayer. Instead, Aniumaru found comfort and compassion. As he lay in his hammock, thinking over what had happened, he saw Jesus in the uda walking toward him. He said Jesus was picking his way through the hammocks, but he wasn't looking at any of the other Suruwahá; he was looking straight at Aniumaru.

"His eyes were like fire and his hair was very black," he said.

"What are you doing here?" Aniumaru asked Jesus.

"I came to see you," he replied, and then walked away.

A little while later Aniumaru fell asleep and had a dream where Jesus took him to heaven. He described in great detail what he saw. He said heaven had a big river, and you could see the horizon for miles around. The area surrounding the river is a lush and fruitful garden, with small palm trees at the water's edge where there are the souls of those rescued by Jesus. There is the sound of women pounding corn in the background, filling the air with music. (The sound of pounding corn signifies abundance.) On the river, angels are paddling in canoes, paddling in tune with the rhythm of heaven, with the feathers behind their ears dancing to the music as in a heavenly choreography.

JASIIRI was the oldest woman in the tribe. She must have been about a hundred years old; her skin was like crumpled paper, and she had no teeth. She couldn't do much, but she would lie in her hammock or hobble around the fire helping to prepare food. Her eyesight was failing, but she was still strong.

Jasiiri's daughter, Siubuka, had been the one to give me the sukady to cover myself when I first entered the tribe. Jasiiri was very wise and knew all the history of the Suruwahá. A couple of times the Suruwahá took her deep into the jungle and abandoned her there to die. Each time Suzuki trekked to the place they had left her and carried her home on his back, often walking for hours. When they returned, Suzuki sweating and exhausted from the journey, the Suruwahá laughed. They were not angry, but they just couldn't see the point of keeping her alive.

One year when none of us were with the tribe, Jasiiri was taken off into the jungle. This time she didn't return.

When Siubuka got old and sick with a disease of the lungs, she didn't want to die the same way her mother had. She asked Suzuki to take her to the city. She was such a good woman; everyone admired her for her bravery and intelligence. Suzuki agreed to take her to Porto

Velho. Her grandson Naru carried her on his back all the way to the place where we would meet the plane.

Naru was eighteen at the time. Everyone told him he was crazy and should leave her. Years before, he had given her poison to encourage her to commit suicide before she got too old. She didn't take it. Since then he had been touched by Jesus and had seen how Suzuki used to carry Jasiiri. Now he was not ashamed to carry his grandmother, despite the ridicule. When he returned to the tribe, he proudly showed his bruises and scratches from carrying Siubuka. She died in a hospital fifteen days later with Suzuki at her side, singing and praying with her as he held her hands. She was the first Suruwahá to not be abandoned in old age.

IKIJI, whose wife, Siraki, had been healed of malaria, was a very intelligent young man and always curious about Jesus. Sometimes if he was upset and was tempted to commit suicide, he would come to us.

"Please ask Jesus to take my sadness away," he would ask.

We would blow on him, as was expected, all the time praying for God to meet him.

One day Suzuki and I went to our house to do some work on translating the Bible into Suruwahá. We invited Ikiji to join us so we could test out our translation on him and see if he understood. Suzuki started with the story of creation and some of the promises of Jesus. Ikiji listened intently right to the end.

"That's not true. It didn't happen," he said finally.

"It is true," I replied and started telling him the story of Aniumaru seeing Jesus.

"No, he was lying," said Ikiji adamantly.

"He wasn't lying. His eyes were shining as he told me," I replied.

I don't know why I used the words "his eyes were shining," but it must have been God because it made Ikiji sit up and take notice.

"Really? His eyes were shining?" asked Ikiji.

"Yes!" I said.

Later I understood that the Suruwahá feel they can tell if a person is lying just by looking at their eyes. If the eyes are opaque, that person is dishonest, but if they are shining, they are telling the truth.

Suddenly Ikiji looked at all we were saying in a new light.

"It must be true then," he said and walked into the night.

We heard him singing outside our house for a long time. After about an hour and a half, he came back in and told us he had been singing songs to Jesus.

"If I was Aniumaru and I had just seen Jesus, this is what I would sing," he said, and proceeded to sing a beautiful song with a haunting melody. He was composing the words and music off the top of his head.

That night Suzuki and I prayed for Ikiji, that he wouldn't have to sing about someone else's experiences but would have his own encounter with God to sing about.

The next morning when we woke, Ikiji asked that we bring a tape recorder; he wanted us to record some of the songs he had in his heart. We had a little minidisc recorder and set it up. This time Ikiji was singing about himself. We never learned exactly what happened in the night, but Ikiji had had an experience of Jesus and was singing about it. One very poetic song I remember was about heaven. Ikiji sang of the angels paddling in a river in heaven; they moved in a melodic rhythm and had feather earrings that danced in their ears in the same melodic way. Ikiji's words were so symbolic and so cultural to the Suruwahá.

Another song spoke about Jesus's blood being the price He paid for our souls, and another was a beautiful description of how the angels adore Jesus in heaven. Today the tribe still uses his songs to worship God.

THE BEAUTIFUL SONGS and touching stories continued. Suzuki and I continued to wait and wonder: how could we best address these precious followers of Jesus? In the end it would be Kuzari, one of the Suruwahá, who gave us the answer.

Kuzari was the joker of the tribe; he was always making people laugh. One evening Suzuki and I were worshipping at the center of the uda. Kuzari started mimicking us; he would raise his hands in the air as we were doing. He had painted his body and put feathers around his sukady. Everyone was laughing at him, including Suzuki and me. He had a gift for making people laugh.

"What if he really had an experience of Jesus? It would be so powerful," I said to Suzuki.

Suzuki agreed. He went over to where twenty-year-old Kuzari was dancing and started praying for him. Suzuki was standing behind

Kuzari with his hands on his head. Suddenly Kuzari fell to the floor under the power of the Holy Spirit. We kept praying, knowing God was touching him.

After a while he got up with a big smile on his face.

"I'm Jesus's *bahi*," he said.

Among the Suruwahá, when you kill an animal, it is your bahi. It belongs to you, but it also relates to death—what you own has to die before it is yours. Kuzari was saying he belonged to Jesus; he had died and was now in Jesus.

Kuzari then went to his hammock and fell into a deep sleep. The next morning we asked what had happened.

"Jesus came and touched me. I was so weak, I had to go straight to my hammock. I couldn't even sniff my tobacco," he said.

After that experience Kuzari completely changed. He would praise and worship God every morning. Kuzari had had a hard life. He was an orphan, and when he was eleven he was made to look after his sick baby niece who was also an orphan. It was meant as a punishment, because he was often very naughty. No one helped him with the little girl. He tried very hard to keep her alive, but after a couple of weeks, she died in his arms.

After his experience in the uda, Jesus started to heal his pain, and Kuzari became a new man. From then on we called those who knew Jesus *Jasiuwa Bahi*: the Suruwahá who belong to Jesus Christ. It was a description they understood completely.

PART FOUR

Hope in the Amazon

THIRTEEN

Hakani

SUZUKI AND I were with the Suruwahá when a baby Indian girl was born into the Suruwahá family of Dihiji, Bujini, and their four sons. Their life in the tribe had been eventful and difficult. The father, Dihiji, had been respected as the second-best hunter in the tribe, while Bujini, the mother, had encountered hardship and tribal pressure around the birth of her fourth son, Niawi.

Initially, Dihiji and Bujini's tribal community had rejoiced at Niawi's birth. But when he was a year old, the people started to notice that there was something wrong with him; he wasn't a normal, healthy baby. Bujini noticed that his movements were slow and that he didn't cry like other babies, but in fear she tried to hide it.

"He has no soul. You have to kill him," the villagers said to Dihiji and Bujini. But the couple loved their little boy and didn't want to kill him. They tried to hide him from the others and keep out of people's way. Both Dihiji and Bujini became withdrawn and depressed; they were under so much pressure to kill the child. The Suruwahá believe that if a child has any deformity it doesn't have a soul and therefore has to be killed. If the child is not buried alive, poisoned, or abandoned in the jungle, it will bring bad luck on the tribe.

From then on, whenever anything went wrong in the tribe, it was blamed on Niawi. Suzuki and I contacted the government department concerned with the health of Indians and told them of the situation, asking them to bring a doctor to help. We filmed the boy and took photos, taking them to doctors in the city and friends in São Paulo, but no one could diagnose what was wrong without seeing him. Dihiji and Bujini were very depressed. I watched them constantly, as I knew they would be tempted to commit suicide.

But then Bujini became pregnant with her fifth child, the child who would eventually become my daughter. Bujini was so afraid that the family was cursed because of her ill son and that the curse would repeat itself in the next child. I was very close to Bujini all through the pregnancy. Suzuki and I hung our hammocks next to her kahu and kept an eye on the family.

Bujini was due to deliver her baby, and when I watched her slowly get up from her hammock and walk into the jungle on the morning of July 9, 1995, I knew that birth was imminent.

A Suruwahá woman gives birth alone. It is a very private thing. After the birth she cuts the umbilical cord with a knife, buries the placenta, then brings the baby back to the village. Sometimes the mother does not bring the baby back. If the baby is a third girl, or if the mother is unmarried, the newborn is buried alive or left to die of exposure.

In this case, thirty minutes later Bujini returned, carrying a baby girl. Bujini climbed into her hammock and lay with her infant. It was a sacred time and no one disturbed them, not even Dihiji. Bujini cleaned her baby and lovingly shaved all the hair of her eyebrows and cut the hair on her head short, as is the custom. She then burned the belly button with a hot stick to prevent infection.

After birthing four sons, the family was considered blessed to have a daughter. Their first little girl, later named Hakani, was a beautiful infant.

For some reason I had a strong desire to take a photo of the baby. I crept over to the hammock; Bujini watched but didn't stop me. I took a photo and quickly left them. It is the only picture I have of a newborn Suruwahá baby, as we normally always avoid disturbing the mother at such a sacred time.

A couple of hours later, Bujini's mother came to see the baby.

"*Warubani imimizi kugani*," she cooed. Translated, it means "her ears are so beautiful." I was very excited because the way she said it was a new grammatical construction; I quickly grabbed my notebook to record it.

Bujini and Dihiji were so happy that they momentarily forgot about the pressure to kill their youngest son. All the older boys—Aruwaji, Ahidi, and Bibi—doted on their sister. Niawi was nearly three when his little sister was born. He was loved by his parents and growing fat on the food they gave him, but he could not walk.

The Suruwahá never name their children right away. They wait for something to happen that will mark the baby's life or speak of the child's character, and then they give the name. Bujini later named her daughter Hakani, which means "smile." She said she gave her this name because she was such a happy baby.

Everything changed when Hakani was about two years old. Her parents realized she had the same problems as her brother Niawi. She was not developing properly. This was too much for Bujini and Dihiji. Many times they both tried to take the poison to kill themselves. One evening we were all singing and dancing with the children in the center of the uda. Suddenly Uniai, Bujini's sister, came running, saying that the couple had taken poison. Immediately I called Suzuki. We were told Bujini and Dihiji had run into the jungle in different directions, so Suzuki went with the men after Dihiji, while I went with some women after Bujini. I was frantically running with my flashlight, but I didn't know the way and was getting lost. Finally I gave my light to some girls, and they kept running after Bujini.

Dihiji and Bujini were both found and brought back to the uda; their relatives tried to make them vomit by putting pineapple leaves and soap water down their throats. I held Bujini's hair back, trying to keep her mouth open so we could make her vomit. I remember watching their three oldest boys that night. They lay on their hammocks staring at the ceiling, not moving, as if frozen in fear. They didn't want to see their parents dying, even though they knew it was inevitable. But by a miracle we were able to save both Dihiji and Bujini. It was only their family that tried to save them; the rest of the tribe stayed away. This was because Dihiji had lost respect on account of his disabled children.

The next day they were weak but alive. Bujini even complained she had a headache because I had pulled her hair back too tightly. But they were both touched by the efforts we had made to save them. It is sign of love and respect if family tries to bring back those who have taken the poison.

A few evenings later, everyone was in the uda that Dihiji had built. Suddenly a huge storm blew up, and I was terrified. I hated thunder and lightning. The wind was whistling through the longhouse, and lightning flashed every few minutes. I was trying to cook a small fish for Suzuki and me, but I could hardly concentrate with the rain lashing down. The Suruwahá think that the lightning and thunder are an angry spirit; it is very dangerous and could strike you down if you are cursed. All the men went to the center of the uda with their machetes, knives, and any tools they had and started shouting and banging the poles of the hut, trying to make a louder noise than the thunder to scare the spirit away. Suddenly there was a huge gust of wind; it felt like the longhouse was being taken up.

The next thing I remember was being flung outside the uda as the roof caved in, crashing to the ground

"Suzuki!" I screamed in fear. Everyone was under the uda; they were surely dead. A few of the parents had had time to throw their small children outside, and there were a couple of others standing with me looking at the collapsed uda in shock. There was complete silence, but after a while the trapped people started to find openings in the thatch to get out. We could hardly see a thing in the darkness. As soon as people started moving, those watching began screaming and crying, looking for their lost children. It was a terrible night, but no one had been killed; only a few had broken bones. When I saw Suzuki poke his head out of the thatch, I shouted with joy and ran to him. He had tried to save our belongings, but a beam had fallen just next to him, trapping our things.

We spent hours trying to help those who had been hurt. The rain was torrential, so we all ran to another uda to take shelter until morning.

By dawn the storm had passed, and the damage was surveyed. Because Dihiji's uda was the one that had been destroyed, the other Indians blamed Niawi and Hakani for the disaster. They would mutter to one another and point to the children, saying that they must die because they were cursed. The women would bang logs with their machetes, showing what should be done to the children. The air was oppressive with their accusation.

Despite everything, Dihiji and Bujini could not kill their little children. They were ostracized from the rest of the village. It was terrible to watch.

A couple of months later, Suzuki and I had to leave to go to Porto Velho to teach at a Cross-Cultural Training School. We still only had one canoe at that time. It took two days to hike to where it was moored and then paddle to where we would be picked up by a plane at the Deni village. We would be gone for a long time, and it would be two weeks before another missionary came to take our place in the interim.

While we were away, Dihiji and Bujini both succeeded in committing suicide. They had felt it was their only option. The villagers all grieved for the couple, even though they had been so angry with them. They blamed the children, not the parents. Hakani and Niawi's lives were now even more at risk.

Moses and Lucilia had taken our place in the tribe with their two small daughters, Esther and Lidia. They arrived to find Dihiji and Bujini dead.

A couple of days later, some of the villagers told Aruwaji, the oldest brother, who was about fifteen, to kill his little brother and sister. They said that if it weren't for the children, his parents would be alive—that they were no better than animals. Full of emotion from his parents' deaths, Aruwaji did what the villagers wanted. Hakani was two and a half, and Niawi was five. Aruwaji hit them both over the head with the back of a machete to knock them out. He then dug a hole close to the house, which is where they bury animals, instead of a proper burial setting. But after he put Hakani in the hole, she suddenly woke up and started screaming, the blood from the machete wound pouring down her head.

Waking up saved her, and she was taken out of the hole. But Niawi was still unconscious and was buried under the dirt. People said that for hours afterwards they could hear Niawi trying to call out. He had woken up too, but it was too late and he suffocated.

Bujini's father decided to look after his little granddaughter. Everyone told him he was wrong to do it; she should be left to die because she was an animal with no soul. He tried to ignore their words but eventually gave in to the pressure.

One morning as Hakani was sleeping, he took out his bow and arrow and shot her just below the left shoulder, crying as he did it. He then went to take some poison; he could not live with what had happened.

WE HEARD ABOUT the deaths upon our return to the tribe. Hakani, by a miracle, did not die; she was kept at the edge of the uda or in the bushes nearby. Her wound got infected and no one cared for her. She was left to sit on the ground.

Sadly, we witnessed a lot of this. We tried to help Hakani many times, but the Indians would not let us. All the food we had came from the tribe, and every time we tried to feed Hakani, they would take the food and tell us that it was theirs, not ours. The food we brought from the city in the canoe was used in the outpost, two days away from the Suruwahá huts. Our hike from the outpost to the tribe allowed us to carry no more than a three-day food supply. The reason for this was practical: we also had to carry our hammocks, flashlights and batteries, medicines, basic hygiene supplies, material for studying the language, and our Bibles. With all this in our backpacks, plus a grueling hike through dense forest, up and down many hills and across flooded areas where water and mud covered half of our bodies, it was impossible to carry more food.

Many times we asked the Indian leaders if we could bring Hakani out of the tribe for medical care, but they wouldn't let us. We knew well the government's position of noninterference; if we antagonized the Indians by removing Hakani against their will, we would be jailed and accused of kidnapping. At the very least, we were still foreigners, dependent on the Suruwahá to remain with the tribe. They had adopted us and were sharing generously. We depended on them for our survival.

For three more years this was Hakani's life. The only thing that kept her going was her older brother Bibi. He would forage in the jungle by day and sneak food to her in the night so no one would know. But people guessed and shouted at him to let his sister die.

Hakani was never given a hammock, but sometimes in the night when everyone was asleep, Bibi would lift her up into his own; it was the only comfort she had. She was treated as a dog and beaten every day by the children. They would burn her with hot coals, and pee into a pineapple bowl, which they would then make her drink. Whenever anyone walked past where she lay, they insulted her.

"You made your parents die. You have no soul—you are not a person. Why don't you die?" they would say.

Suzuki and I did what we could, but it was not nearly enough. I tried to give her food, but whenever I did, it was snatched out of her hands by the Indians. Time and time again we asked government workers if we could take Hakani out of the tribe, but they said no, we had to respect the culture. We felt helpless, desperate for the life of this poor little girl.

It was very hard for me. I cried many times for Hakani's life and felt totally hopeless. I would spend hours in my hammock strategizing about how I could hide her in the jungle, complete the two-day trek to our outpost house, and take her to the city for medical care. Then I would fantasize about what I would do in the city to convince the authorities it was not kidnapping. After hours of fantasizing, I would give up and cry alone in the darkness. The consequences of my taking Hakani out of the jungle would be serious. Suruwahá reactions were totally unpredictable; Bibi could take poison, or the tribe could pursue us into the jungle. And even if we made it to the city, FUNAI would never accept this. We would go to jail. I had given up hope, and I was only waiting for the day Hakani would die in the tribe.

Hakani couldn't walk; all she could do was sit on the dirt and endure her torment. No one helped her to go into the jungle to relieve herself. The Suruwahá hate all excretion and leave their clearing to do what they need to do in the jungle. Hakani could not move, so she had feces all over herself. Every time someone saw this, they would beat her on the small of her back with a machete handle. They even cut her with machetes, and she still has the scars on her back, head, and face today.

She was so hungry that she would eat the insects crawling around her. Suruwahá hate insects, so they were even more disgusted with her for doing this, but she had no other option.

Sometime after Hakani's fifth birthday, I was sure she would die. She was still the size of a baby, and her skin was black and infected. She was emaciated, with a large extended stomach. The Suruwahá didn't call her Hakani, but Jeweke, which is a derogatory word meaning "ugly small thing."

At that time the Suruwahá tribe was divided, living in two udas separated by jungle trails. The uda Suzuki and I worked in was not Hakani's. One day the villagers started to say Jeweke was dead; she was lying lifelessly on the ground. I was so sad. I went over see her. Her body was motionless, but when I came over, she looked at me with her big black eyes and my heart stood still. She was alive. A few hours later Bibi strapped her to his back and brought her over to our uda. He didn't say a word; just looked at me, his eyes communicating more than he could ever say. He then left her with us on the ground at the edge of the uda and walked into the jungle. Suzuki went over to see if she was alive and found she was still breathing. With Moses he took her to the river to wash away all the dirt and filth.

We believe that it was because Uhuzai and Ania had given a favorable account of life outside the jungle that Bibi gave Hakani to us. He knew we could take her out and she would be okay.

Lucilia and I wanted to take care of her, but there was something in her that made it difficult to go near Hakani; I don't fully understand what it was. At first I thought I had the reaction because I wasn't a mother and didn't have maternal instincts, but Lucilia was the same. Hakani had been told all her life that she was a curse and worthless, and this had a deep effect on every area of her life. She had stopped growing and stopped smiling. She was like a living corpse. We put her in Lucilia's daughter's hammock and decided to pray all night for her life. It was unlikely that she would survive the night, but we had to try.

We went to the middle of the uda and cried out to God, every once in a while going to check on her to see if there was any improvement. Her tummy was huge and hard with her tiny legs and arms sticking out. She was barely breathing. The Suruwahá thought we were crazy to care for this girl. They told us to leave her to die.

As dawn was beginning to break, we all decided to get a bit of sleep. When I woke up I went over to where Hakani was lying and screamed in shock. The whole hammock was covered in feces; the volume was more than her entire body. It was disgusting—full of feathers, bones, sticks, whatever she had eaten. The Suruwahá heard my scream and came over to look; when they saw her, they simply laughed and walked away.

Suzuki took her to the stream to wash her and saw that her belly had shrunk; she seemed to have more life in her. We realized she had stopped herself from having bowel movements because every time she did, she was beaten. So her body was full of feces, and if it hadn't come out, it would have killed her.

Over the next couple of days, she seemed to improve quickly, but for a week Lucilia and I still couldn't touch her. Esther patiently fed her corn porridge. At the end of the week, Lucilia, Moses, and the girls were leaving, and Suzuki was taking them in the canoe. I would be left alone with Hakani and I was terrified. I was sure she would die, she was so weak. I didn't know if I could look after her. But somehow we both made it through until Suzuki returned.

We spent two weeks with her in the uda and then two weeks at the outpost we had built with John and Denise. One day when I was alone with her, I was trying to feed her. By a miracle I suddenly remembered her mother had called her Hakani, even though the villagers had never called her that, and I knew her as Jeweke.

"Hakani," I said, testing the name out.

Suddenly she looked at me. Her eyes sparkled and she smiled.

"Hakani!" I repeated over and over again, and my heart melted as she responded.

FOURTEEN

A Child by the End of the Year

HAKANI AND I started to bond at that point. It had been so hard before. She had acted and looked like an animal. For the whole first month she had never looked at us in the eyes. She would snatch the food we gave her and turn her back to us. She was fragile but very angry. She wanted our food but was not open to love. When I said her name, a crack appeared in the wall and a little bit of light shone in.

We had thought she had severe mental problems since she had no expression on her face. At that point I had no thought in my head that I might keep her. If we kept her out of the tribe, I was sure the government would take her away, so I started writing the main parts of her story to give to the nurses so they might have compassion on her.

We knew we had to get Hakani out of the jungle to see a doctor. We took her to the Deni tribe by canoe. From there, the missionaries Lourdes and Elton Chaves (a couple who helped us after our boat sank in the river) took her by plane to Lábrea, where they met Moses. Moses accompanied Hakani to the hospital. Suzuki and I stayed with the tribe in case they reacted badly to her leaving. After a week Moses was given an official document by the government, giving YWAM guardianship of Hakani. He flew her to meet us in Porto Velho.

We spent three months with Hakani in Porto Velho. When we brought her in, she weighed only seven kilos (15 pounds) and was 69 cm (27 inches). Her pediatrician, Dr. José Roberto Vasques, wouldn't charge us for his work. He saw Hakani every two weeks and diagnosed her with congenital hypothyroidism, which, because it had been left untreated, had caused cretinism—severely stunted physical and mental growth. At five and a half years old, Hakani was the size of a toddler.

Hakani was also evaluated by a neurologist, who did not give us a positive prognosis.

"I am sorry, but she will never be able to walk," he said. "I am surprised she has survived without treatment for so long. The best you can hope for is that she might be able to feed herself one day."

I never believed the neurologist's words. I knew Hakani would not only be able to walk and talk, but much more.

We spent the last nine months of 2001 in São Paulo while Hakani received treatment in the hospital there. In that time she improved dramatically; she even started to walk.

When we returned to Porto Velho, I took Hakani to see Dr. José Roberto because she had the flu. I carried her into his room and then placed her on the floor where she started walking around.

Dr. José looked from me to Hakani in shock. "She's walking," he gasped.

"Yes!" I replied joyfully before apologizing that I hadn't told him of her progress earlier.

Tears fell down Dr. José's cheeks as he watched Hakani.

"You don't understand. The medicine she is taking would never have done this," he said.

"Well, she has had a lot of prayer too," I replied.

"And a lot of love," he said, smiling.

The next day was "March for Jesus" in Porto Velho, and I took Hakani to be part of it. We were with a big group of YWAMers. They all cried as they saw Hakani. The girl who doctors said would never walk was now walking for Jesus.

It took her longer to learn to speak, but that could have been because she had to learn Portuguese, a whole new language. After a year we decided to take Hakani back to the tribe.

We spent only a week in the village and the rest of the time in our house, two days' walk from the tribe. The reaction of the people when they saw Hakani was complete amazement.

"*Zama ini diumurini hinsi kieny, zama ini karujini jahuruwaguani,*" they said—"She was like garbage, but now she has become beautiful like a princess. She is someone of value."

The people grieved for her buried brother, realizing that he could have been the same as Hakani if he had not been buried. Boys are of higher value than girls to the Suruwahá, so they felt their mistake deeply.

The biggest impact Hakani had was on the mothers in the tribe. They realized that they did not have to bury their babies; that there were people in the city who could help. Hakani's grandmother cried and hugged her, saying over and over again, "My daughter is a person, and she is beautiful."

When we went back to our home after the week with the tribe, Bibi came with us. He would look at Hakani without saying a word. He stayed for a few days and then walked back to the village, content his little sister was alive and being looked after.

Hakani had seemed happy with the tribe, but I noticed when we were there that she didn't seem to understand as much when I spoke to her, either in Portuguese or Suruwahá. When we got home, she stopped talking altogether for three months. It was the only way her body could express the deep emotional pain she had been under. As the memories came back, her ability to speak stopped. (When she did start to talk again, she developed a stammer that was only rectified in 2006.)

I realized when Hakani stopped speaking that it had been too soon to take her back. I decided then not to take her back again until I was sure she would be able to cope.

IT WAS WHEN Hakani first arrived in Porto Velho that I knew she would be my daughter. Suzuki and I had assumed we would not have children because of the life we led, and I had been content with that. But then in May 2000, six months before Bibi dropped Hakani outside our uda, we had an American pastor named Mike Shea staying with us in Porto Velho.

One morning over breakfast, he told us he felt God was saying we would have a child by the end of the year.

"That's impossible!" I laughed.

I was perfectly content without children and we weren't trying. Even if I got pregnant that day, the baby would be born nine months later, which would not be the same year.

Mike was very humble: "Okay, maybe I heard wrong. I'll go and pray about it some more."

A few days later he came back even more adamant.

"I really think God is saying you will have a child by the end of the year, and it will be a blessing to the Suruwahá people," he said.

Suzuki and I thanked him, and I promptly forgot all about it. If God wanted to give us a child this year, He could do it, but I could not fathom how it would happen.

In November of that year, as I was sitting with Hakani in the hospital, I remembered the prophecy. This was the child God had spoken about. I knew then that she would live and be a blessing to her people. Becoming her mother was the most natural thing. Soon all my thoughts were filled with her. I couldn't sleep if she was ill. I wanted to adopt her. It took Suzuki a couple more months to feel the same way. He was worried about how our lives would change.

"She is my daughter. I will make any change for her," I said.

Suzuki agreed and fell in love with her as much as I had.

We visited a judge, Dr. Waldecy, in Porto Velho and told him Hakani's story. He was very sympathetic and gave us papers of guardianship. But we wanted to be her parents, to have legal custody. We approached FUNAI, who said they would send anthropologists into the jungle to find out what really happened, but they never did and therefore could not provide a document proving Hakani's parents were dead. The adoption process dragged on.

About three years later Kuzari, one of the Suruwahá, had to come to Porto Velho for medical treatment of minor brain damage that he had suffered in a suicide attempt. We realized he had been there when Dihiji and Bujini died, so he could verify that they were no longer alive.

The judge arranged an official meeting to interview Kuzari. I convinced Kuzari to put clothes on, and we walked into the courtroom with Moses as a translator. The Suruwahá have no idea of formalities, and Kuzari was immediately amazed by the air conditioning in the room. He put his arms in the air, breathing in the coolness.

"It's so wonderful," he said over and over again, before lying down on top of the judge's desk and basking in the cool breeze from the air conditioning machine! The judge didn't quite know what to make of him, but he had a sense of humor and waited for Kuzari to finish reveling in the cool air and tell his description of events. Kuzari confirmed that Hakani's parents were dead. (Two more years passed before we were officially seen as Hakani's parents. In 2005, after five years of struggle with the government, we were finally granted permanent custody and were able to proceed with the adoption process.)

WE WEREN'T THE ONLY ONES to adopt a Suruwahá child. Lucilia and Moses also adopted. Lucilia was a teacher and had been a missionary with the Parakanã tribe, teaching in a small school. She had been expelled by the government for living with the Indians, and the federal police had come into the tribe to remove her. She moved to the Porto Velho YWAM base, where she met Moses, married, and birthed her two little girls, Esther and Lidia.

In 2002 Moses, Lucilia, and the girls were with the Suruwahá alone. There was a young girl who was pregnant, and they knew she was planning to abandon the baby because she wasn't married. They stayed very close to her hammock and kept an eye on her, hoping to save the child when it was born. They would have to be very quick, or the pregnant girl's father would kill the baby. She was only fifteen, but she had already been pregnant by another man and her father had killed that baby. Lucilia knew how important it was to stay near if they were going to save the baby. But then one day they were praying and felt God clearly tell them to leave the tribe and camp at a place where they were planning to build a house, about five hours' walk away.

"But, Lord, if we leave, the baby will die," Lucilia pleaded.

Trust Me, was all she heard back, and she knew they had to obey.

So the family traveled to the location of their new home, praying for the life of the unborn baby all the way.

A week or so later, one of the sisters of the pregnant girl came running through the jungle to where they were camped. She told them what had happened. Her sister had gone into the jungle to give birth and had abandoned the child. But her two sisters, aged ten and eleven, followed her and hid the baby under some leaves so their father wouldn't come and kill it. They left the umbilical cord attached. The sisters then went to find Moses and Lucilia to tell them what had happened.

Tears streamed down Lucilia's cheeks as she heard the story, and Moses left to find the child. He trekked all day through the jungle and finally found her. She was still alive; miraculously she hadn't been eaten by an animal, which often happens. By this time it was dark, so Moses cut the baby's umbilical cord, slept with the child in his arms, and left at first light. He made it back to Lucilia at the end of the next day.

A couple of months before, Lucilia had stopped breastfeeding Lidia. On the day Moses brought back the abandoned baby Lucilia felt milk filling her breasts and she started lactating again. It was a miracle and saved the life of the child. Lucilia was able to feed her and she quickly grew stronger and healed from the insect bites that covered her body.

Word soon got out that the baby was alive, and the sisters came to see the baby.

"She's alive, she's alive," beamed Lucilia when she saw them.

"Her name will be Harani," said one of the girls, meaning "she is alive."

Two years later, Harani's mother committed suicide when she became pregnant again. The girl's father had said that if she had another baby, he would not only kill it, he would cut it up.

Harani was left an orphan. Moses and Lucilia began the process of adoption since no one in the tribe wanted her. They went to the same judge who had helped us with Hakani, and Harani became their daughter.

FIFTEEN

Teaching and Training

NOW THAT WE WERE SO CLOSE to becoming a family of three, we had to decide what we were going to do. Hakani was getting stronger every day and no longer needed so much medical attention, but we knew we could not go back to the Suruwahá with her yet. We would have to wait many years until she would be emotionally ready. I didn't want to cause her any more harm. After prayer and discussion we felt we should go to the Sateré-Mawé. I already knew the language, so it would be easier for us as a family.

Much had happened since I had last been to Atuka. Isabel and Kadete had died of old age, and Christians from the village had moved to other villages and were spreading the gospel.

At first we moved to the YWAM base in Maués, a short boat trip from the tribe. When we started visiting old friends with Hakani, we realized the need for teaching and training among the Sateré Christians. So in September 2002 we planned a three-day conference to train and encourage the Sateré.

It was amazing to see the Indians coming up the river in their canoes with their families to attend the conference. Around one hundred and fifty Indians came, all staying at the base, stringing their hammocks in different buildings.

When I saw the boats arriving with the Indians singing worship songs in Sateré, I felt very emotional. There were people coming whom I hadn't seen for years. I could hardly wait. All the memories of my years in Atuka and Monjuru flooded back, and the hardships seemed worth it, seeing all these happy, praising Christians.

I was scheduled to preach since I spoke their language, but from the moment I saw the Indians in their boats, I lost my voice. In the end the leader of the base preached in Portuguese and had a translator. We were giving missionary vision to the Sateré—explaining the heart of Jesus to go out to the lost and tell them the good news. Many Sateré were deeply touched and came forward to give their lives to missions. It was a powerful time; we felt the presence of God strongly and knew He was doing a deep work among the Indians.

After the success of the conference, we felt God was asking us to invest more in the Sateré-Mawé, so we planned for the first tribal Discipleship Training School to start in February 2003. It wouldn't look like anything we had ever done before. We talked to the Sateré Christians and they all wanted it to take place in the jungle, as there would be too many distractions in a village. We realized we would have to build a whole new village just for the course.

A team was gathered from Porto Velho and set out with pots and pans, hammocks, and all the equipment we would need. We searched for and found a perfect spot, close to the river and with a natural spring that we could drink from. Much later I realized it was the place where Daisy and I were saved by Urbano, but thankfully I didn't remember at the time.

There were eleven Sateré-Mawé men doing the course, but they were not alone. They had brought their entire families with them. We had to build a village for almost eighty people.

The first day we all sat on logs by the water's edge and worshipped the Lord for bringing us this far. God spoke to us powerfully, that many missionaries would go from this place and that they would not only go to other Indians, but to the nations.

Excited, we got to work building the village the next day. We built six thatched huts, avoiding snakes and scorpions as we cleared the ground. In twenty days it was all done, which must have been some kind of record.

When the DTS actually started, the days were interrupted by the students going hunting or fishing for food. We had brought some rice, beans, and coffee with us, but the rest we got from the jungle.

Very quickly we learned that the Sateré do not react well to planning. If I told them the night before what they would be doing the next day, they didn't like it.

"How do I know what will happen tomorrow or how I will feel when I get out of my hammock?" they would say.

We had thought we were pretty flexible before the DTS, but the Sateré brought the need for flexibility to a whole new level. One day Suzuki was teaching in one of the huts. Suddenly the students started getting distracted; they were grabbing things out of the air.

"What are you catching?" Suzuki asked, confused.

They explained there were flying termites in the air which are delicious to eat. Soon the lecture was disbanded, and all of us were running about catching the termites. That evening we feasted on the catch, frying them over the open fire.

Each evening we would sit around the fires in the middle of the huts, praying and worshipping. The Sateré were so hungry for God.

For the outreach phase of the school we traveled to different Sateré-Mawé villages in the area. We went to Monjuru, and the Indians preached to their own people.

One of the biggest blessings to come out of the first tribal DTS was that the Indians learned how to worship God in their own culture. We were trying to find new ways to explain Biblical principles to them so they would be able to relate.

One day Suzuki was teaching on the story of Jesus washing the disciples' feet and the importance of humility. As he talked, he was multitasking and grinding guaraná seeds. In Sateré culture it is the lowest person present who grinds the seeds. So it was very unusual for Suzuki to be doing it, as he was the leader and teacher in the group. The process of making the guaraná drink is very long and cumbersome. The seeds are first dried, then toasted over a fire, then ground into a thick cream, which is made into a sausage shape. The ground sausage-like substance is left to smoke over a fire for months. It is then ground again with a special rock found only in the river. Finally water is added, and the drink is placed in a large bowl out of which everyone drinks. The process is very formal and every part of the ritual has a deep meaning. Even the way it is ground has significance—it has to be done in a circular clockwise motion, to symbolize uniting all the people in the village.

So as Suzuki was speaking about Jesus washing the disciples' feet, he was slowly grinding the sausage-like substance. Suddenly the students grasped what he was saying and started weeping at the revelation of who Jesus is. Suzuki was demonstrating the humility of Jesus by grinding the fruit. Without realizing it, he had taken on a humble position and served as an example to the tribe.

The Indians were so touched that later they incorporated what they had learned into the liturgy of their services. The drink made from the seeds is called *sapo,* and the Indians use it as their communion wine. It is kept in a bowl in the center of the hut, in the lowest place, and each person who comes to drink from it has to kneel down to pick up the bowl. It is very powerful to see the Sateré-Mawé's own cultural expression of communion.

Our graduation day was overwhelming. The celebrations started at seven in the evening and didn't stop until seven o'clock the next morning.

ONE YEAR LATER we returned to teach a second DTS. After that, three Indian families carried on the training with long-term outreaches in other villages.

The following Christmas, Suzuki and I decided to visit the leader of the whole Sateré-Mawé tribe and honor him with a gift. As we sat outside his house, drinking guaraná together and talking, he suddenly looked at me and asked: "Have you ever forgiven me?"

As he said that, it was as if my eyes were opened, and I immediately recognized him as the Indian who had taken Daisy and me in the small canoe to be gang-raped by the Brazilian laborers.

As the memories came flooding back, I remembered the terror I had felt. This man had sold me more than twenty years previously, and yet here I was in front of him, married and bringing him a gift. Much had happened in those twenty years. He had not only become the chief of the Sateré-Mawé, but had also become a Christian.

"It was you . . ." I gasped, shocked. "You took me to be raped by those sixty men?"

"Sixty-eight," he corrected. "But I saved your life one year later, when you were dying of malaria at Monjuru village."

"That was you too?" I said, the truth slowly becoming clear to me.

"Yes, I almost caused your death, but I also saved your life. Do you forgive me?"

I held no reproach for what he had done. God had healed my heart from each experience.

"Yes, I forgive you," I said.

Suzuki had no idea what was going on. I turned to him and took his hand.

"I will tell you all about it when we get home!" I said.

It was a shocking revelation, and the last thing I had expected when visiting the chief, but I knew that I really had forgiven him in my heart, and I thanked God that he was a different man from the one I once knew.

THE INDIANS HAD LEARNED A LOT about caring for and serving others through the DTS programs; they had had a heart transformation, and the fruit was amazing.

One of those couples, Chagas and Celina, were touched by the need to help their people who had left the jungle searching for jobs and a better life. Many of them had succumbed to drink and drugs. As a result, their children were abandoned on the streets with no hope. Girls as young as ten were selling their bodies for an ice cream. The situation was heartbreaking. Chagas and Celina decided to go back to an area in Maués and minister to the Indians there.

Chagas was the son of Isabel, the woman who had had the dream of our arrival in Atuka. Celina was the daughter of Tomé, who had first told Euci and me about Pastor Jovito. Chagas married Celina when she was thirteen and he was fifteen. They had a deep understanding of God and loved Him with all their hearts. Over the years they had been praying for a way to help their people, but they were so poor themselves that they could hardly feed their five children.

One day Celina and Chagas were praying, and God spoke to them from Isaiah 54:2: "Enlarge the place of your tent, stretch your tent curtains wide, do not hold back; lengthen your cords, strengthen your stakes."

They looked around their tiny house, already full to bursting with their family. Outside there was a small piece of land.

"We could build a hut and teach and feed children there," Celina said excitedly.

"But we don't have any money to build," Chagas reminded her.

When they prayed again, they felt God was saying to go ahead and build the hut. So in obedience they started with all they had. Chagas found some wood from the jungle outside the city and started building the structure. There was no money for the thatch, but Chagas was still working away on the structure in faith that God would do something. Sure enough, one day as Chagas was on the roof, Mark Barnes, an American YWAM missionary, walked past.

"Hi, Chagas, what are you doing up there?" he shouted up.

"I am building a school," Chagas said.

"I want to give you the money to finish it," Mark said, perhaps knowing how poor Chagas and Celina were.

Chagas couldn't contain his excitement. He jumped off the roof and ran to tell Celina the good news. Within a month they were feeding thirty children two meals a day and teaching them to read and write.

After the second DTS we decided to go and support Celina and Chagas in Maués by helping to raise funds for them. Their ministry has continued to grow, and they are transforming the community they live in. Their nineteen-year-old daughter Meire did a DTS in São Paulo and has now returned to help her parents as principal of the school. The school has been so successful that it was televised nationally as an example of a community-based social project. When Chagas and Celina stretched their dwelling wide, God stretched it wider.

SIXTEEN

Families in Need

THE YEAR WAS 2005. The phone started ringing at the Maués YWAM base, interrupting my thoughts. My head was caught up with ideas of how to support the fledgling ministry among the Indian children in the city.

"*Bom dia*," I said as I picked up the phone.

"Márcia, eight Suruwahá are at the base in Porto Velho. Can you and Suzuki come and help?" our friend Moses said on the other end of the line. Immediately my thoughts clicked into the present.

Moses explained that there were two families with sick children and they wanted medical help. I told him I would let him know as soon as possible, and then ran to find Suzuki.

We had been due to fly to Norway to teach in a linguistics school, but the Suruwahá needed us. We decided we would travel with Hakani to Porto Velho to help Moses and arranged for our linguistics students from Europe to join us there, where they would receive teaching and help us care for the Indians.

On our arrival we were reacquainted with our friend Muwaji, a twenty-eight-year-old widow. Muwaji had a nine-year-old son, Ahuhari, and a new little girl, Iganani, who was sick with suspected cerebral palsy.

In previous years Muwaji and I had often talked of ways to save babies whom we knew were going to be killed. She had helped save several children in the past. When she knew a mother was about to give birth, Muwaji would watch to see when she went into the jungle. If the mother came out without the child, Muwaji would go and find the baby, trim the umbilical cord, and try to protect the child as much as she could. She then went back to the mother and sat close to her in her hammock and started talking about the baby. She would tell the mother she had seen the child, that it was beautiful, it was alive, and needed its mother. More often than not the mother would retrieve her baby. When Niawi, Hakani's brother, had been buried, Muwaji was very distressed. She sat by the grave for hours. She told me she couldn't move as she heard Niawi's muffled cries. As a widow, there was nothing she could do; she was helpless.

Ironically, Muwaji was now in the same predicament. She had become pregnant after her husband died and had given birth to little Iganani. Being unwed and birthing a female were two strikes against her. In this kind of situation, a baby boy might be allowed to survive, but according to tribal custom, Muwaji was required to bury this child. The thought was unbearable.

Unbearable to me too, as my friend told us her story. Before the birth, Muwaji had started feeling contractions and slowly made her way to the jungle. There was no excitement or anticipation; she knew what she had to do. She gave birth to Iganani, left her in the jungle, and made her way back to the village. She lay in her hammock and tried to avoid contact with anyone. But Muwaji's mother saw her distress. She knew how much Muwaji wanted the baby, so defying custom and culture, she went back into the jungle to retrieve Iganani. Bringing her back, she placed the little girl in her daughter's arms. Everyone was telling Muwaji to kill her. Even her son, Ahuhari, was jumping up and down shouting, "Kill her! Kill her!"

Muwaji stood firm for a few months, protecting her little girl, but when Iganani was six months old, Muwaji noticed she couldn't move her arms and legs very well. She was not able to hold things in her hands. There was something wrong with her baby. The rest of the tribe noticed too, and again pressure was put on Muwaji to kill Iganani. No one would talk to her. They whispered behind her back, walking away if she came near.

After a couple of days, it was too much for Muwaji. She was being ostracized by her own people. She decided the only way out was to abandon Iganani.

But as Muwaji lay in her hammock, having left her baby in the jungle for the second time, she could hear Iganani crying out. Muwaji just lay in her hammock, trying to ignore the cries, too petrified to move or feel or do anything. For hours Iganani cried. Finally Muwaji broke. She couldn't do it. She rushed into the jungle to save her daughter. By this time the rats had already gotten to her and were chewing at her legs, but she was alive.

"I cannot kill my baby. I am going to find help for her," Muwaji told the rest of the village when she returned with Iganani in her arms.

THE SECOND FAMILY asking for help was Naru's, the man who, a few years earlier, had carried his elderly grandmother out of the village rather than abandon her to die. He and his wife, Kusiuma, had a three-year-old son, Atiasiu, and a six-month-old baby. From the baby's genitals they could not tell whether the child was a girl or a boy.

Kusiuma had gone into the jungle to give birth and was terrified when she saw what was wrong with her child. She had never seen or heard of anything like it and was so afraid she abandoned the baby in the jungle. She walked back to the village and lay in her hammock, so upset over what had just happened. One of her relatives saw the state she was in, went into the jungle, and brought the baby back, placing it in Kusiuma's arms. This was very unusual among the Suruwahá. Suzuki and I used to do it all the time, and perhaps after seeing Hakani, the relative thought there might be a chance for the baby.

When Naru arrived to inspect his child, he too realized there was something wrong with it and took an arrow to shoot the baby. But as he pulled his arm back to aim the bow and arrow, he started shaking and couldn't go through with it. Both Naru and his wife were crying, knowing they would have to kill the child.

Kuakuai, the chief who had replaced Hamy, saw what was happening. He came over and gave Naru a big sniff of tobacco to calm his nerves.

"You don't have to kill your baby. You can take it to the missionaries," he said.

Moses and Lucilia were in the village at that time, and Moses accompanied Naru and his family to Porto Velho for treatment, on a boat organized by the government. Muwaji would arrive later. (At the last minute Muwaji's son, who didn't want to go, disappeared in the jungle. Devastated, Muwaji had to stay behind until he was found. She thought she had missed her only chance to save her daughter. But a few days later, some government nurses were brought in by helicopter to give vaccinations, and they let Muwaji and her children come back with them to Porto Velho.)

Siagani, the son of the chief, came to support his friend Naru. He was a wonderful man, so humble and clever; the tribe loved him because he reminded them of Hamy. He pretended he needed to come to Porto Velho because of a problem with his teeth, but the truth was he knew Naru would be too scared to leave on his own.

WHEN SUZUKI, HAKANI, AND I arrived in Porto Velho from Maués, the families had already been seen by a doctor. Iganani was diagnosed with cerebral palsy and was scheduled to travel to São Paulo, where more extensive medical facilities would ensure the right treatment. Naru's baby also needed further diagnosis and care.

Moving the families was a challenge. We did not want to force the Indians to come; it had to be their own decision. Suzuki clearly explained the difficulties they would face in São Paulo. When Naru found out he was going to have to travel to an even bigger city, he decided he and his family would not go; they would return to the tribe. It was Siagani who persuaded them to stay. Siagani had the heart of a chief and was very compassionate toward his friends. We were able to obtain government authorization to travel with the Indians and take them on an airplane; it required our payment of $8000 in airfare.

Two days before we arrived in São Paulo, we had nowhere to stay. Every place we tried refused us. They would say yes at first and then discover we had Indians with us and say no. But we kept on trusting God. We felt His direction leading us to go, and finally a Japanese church said we could stay in a camp they had just outside the city.

It could not have been more perfect if we had planned it ourselves. The camp houses were built like Japanese pagodas. They were round, with places for the Suruwahá to hang their hammocks. It was a beautiful area and very peaceful. The camp was surrounded by palm trees and bushes, just what the Suruwahá needed to feel at home. The church also blessed us with plenty to eat, so much that we were giving food away to neighbors.

The medical news was good for Naru and Kusiuma's baby. Tests determined a female gender, and surgery was scheduled to remedy her condition. Naru and Kusiuma rejoiced when they heard the news of the upcoming surgery—their burden lifted, their eyes shining with thanksgiving. They named the baby Tititu which means "sweet little thing."

This bubble of good news burst when an indigenous missionary anthropologist found out we had taken eight Suruwahá to São Paulo. He did not agree with our actions and sent a letter to the federal prosecutor in Manaus, accusing us of kidnapping the Indians.

FUNAI officials told the federal prosecutor they didn't know we had Suruwahá with us in São Paulo. We presented the documents we had been issued but were accused of faking them.

The federal prosecutor began an investigation, speaking first with the director of the hospital where Tititu and Iganani were receiving treatment. This was very intimidating for hospital officials, who told us they would need authorization from the government to continue treatments.

Weeks flew by as officials from FUNASA, Brazil's national health foundation, and hospital authorities surveyed the situation. In the meantime, all medical treatment stopped. Naru was frustrated and disillusioned with how he was treated. He and his wife would cry each night; they missed the tribe and wanted to go home.

"Why are we treated this way? Are the doctors only for outsiders?" he asked.

We had to respect the authorities, but it was a mess. Finally I decided to write an open letter to everyone I knew and include a photo of Tititu, explaining the situation and asking for prayer and help.

The letter spread like wildfire all over Brazil. A Christian anthropologist read it during a university lecture in São Paulo. One of the students knew someone from Globo, Brazil's national television network. He told them the story, and the next thing we knew we were receiving phone calls from *Fantástico*, one of the network's premiere programs. *Fantástico* wanted to interview the Suruwahá, Suzuki and me, and government officials on their program.

We wanted to be wise and knew it wasn't likely that the network would side with missionaries in a possible argument with the government. We were worried that speaking on the program wouldn't help the Suruwahá and that we could be accused not only of kidnapping, but also of exploiting them on national television. We were in a really hard place.

So we cried out to God for wisdom, and He spoke very clearly. He said the Suruwahá are free, not the property of the government; ask them if they want to speak.

So, explaining all the implications, we asked if they wanted to tell their story. They said yes, and we agreed to interpret for them.

The program was broadcast to twenty-five million viewers on a Sunday evening in September 2005. I was so impressed by Naru. He was not intimidated at all and confidently spoke from his heart to the nation of Brazil.

"Please, I need your help," he said. "If you don't help, I will have to go home and kill my daughter and myself. If you do help her, my eyes will only be happiness."

Muwaji said even though she missed the tribe so much, she would spend the rest of her life in the city if she thought it would help her daughter. The public's reaction was very positive.

The next day a national health foundation administrator arrived at the hospital and gave authorization for medical treatment to continue. The forces against us had come off very badly on the show; FUNAI, FUNASA, and the legal officials turned on each other, placing blame. We were glad treatment could continue but were aware of possible consequences. We braced ourselves for a backlash.

Sure enough, the following week *Fantástico* denounced YWAM as a fanatical organization that was destroying the tribes and not respecting the government. This made life difficult not only for YWAM but for all missionaries working with Indians in the Amazon, threatening to expel groups from their work.

At the same time, government authorities moved the eight Suruwahá who were with us into the "Indian House" or *Casa do Índio* (*Casai*) against their will. These houses were established by the ministry of health and were designed to meet the needs of indigenous people while they were outside their villages seeking medical care. Suzuki and I were not allowed to have any contact with the Indians, but since we were the only ones who could speak Suruwahá, we were allowed to serve as interpreters.

A week before this unraveling, we had been in a church service. A congregation member who was a lawyer came up to us and asked if we needed his help. At the time all seemed well, so we said thank you, but we didn't need a lawyer. He gave us his card anyway and told us to call if there were any problems. It was only a couple of days later that we took him up on his offer.

We met our lawyer friend in a local restaurant. He knew of our work and had helped purchase our new boat a few years before. We talked through all the details with him. He had been investigating and told us we were very close to going to prison for the alleged kidnapping of the two Suruwahá families. He advised us to send a letter to the government official who had stated on *Fantástico* that teams working with Amazonian Indians might be expelled. We told him that we still had a team with the Suruwahá and didn't want them to be in trouble. We also wrote that we were concerned that the Suruwahá would try to kill themselves here in São Paulo if the government wouldn't allow our presence; we were their only bridge to the outside world. No one else spoke their language. We registered the letter and made it official, but we never got a reply.

At this point Suzuki and I were still living in the church camp, visiting the Suruwahá in the Indian House every day. Tititu had had the operation after the first *Fantástico* program aired, and her parents were so impressed. Everything went perfectly. They would take off her diaper and show anyone who wanted to see the results. They were ready to go home after a month, but all the paperwork took so long that they weren't given permission to leave until three months later. They had hated every moment in the Casai. No one spoke their language, and they were afraid of the other Indians. However, compared to many Casai, the one in São Paulo was actually quite nice. Six months earlier the government had closed it down because the conditions were so awful; when it reopened it was clean, with only thirty Indians staying there. Still, Naru would tie a knot in the rope of his hammock each day to mark another day gone before they could go home.

Meanwhile, Muwaji had been getting treatment for Iganani, who was improving rapidly. Eventually everyone was allowed to go back to the tribe. The government arranged for four people to travel with the Suruwahá on the flight to Porto Velho, and Suzuki went with them as the interpreter. Both families were only going home for a visit. Iganani needed more medical treatment, and Tititu was going to have a few more tests to make sure everything was okay.

Knowing that they were coming back, we decided that I would stay in São Paulo and rent an apartment with Hakani, awaiting their return.

We waited patiently, and in January 2006 the government sent Suzuki as an interpreter with a group of health care workers to retrieve the families from the village. However, instead of bringing the group back to São Paulo, they were transferred to Manaus. This made no sense to us; the right medical treatment they needed was in the bigger city. The group was housed in a Casai with terrible conditions. Over three hundred Indians were living there, and it was full of disease. The Suruwahá were terrified.

Suzuki was living in the Casai to comfort the Suruwahá and protect them from committing suicide, because they were getting desperate. I moved up to Manaus with Hakani, and we stayed in a mission house nearby. Aji, Muwaji's brother, had come to help as well.

The Suruwahá were angry. They kept bows and arrows with them and didn't trust anyone. But they still found favor in the Casai. The manager of the building was a man named Adilson, and he took a liking to them. He said he was moved by their story and realized how difficult they were finding it to live in the communal bedroom with no windows, and so he let them move into his office. He put hooks on the walls for their hammocks and did what he could to make them happy.

We were supposed to be there for only a week, but twenty days later nothing had changed. Iganani was allowed to go to the hospital twice a week for a fifteen-minute physiotherapy session. In São Paulo she had been given treatment three afternoons a week for the whole afternoon. Muwaji realized it was pointless for her to be there. At the same time, Tititu and her family were not allowed to go back to the tribe, because the authorities said there wasn't a flight for them. The waiting was torturing them.

All the time Suzuki and I were praying and calling out to God. We were in the middle of a battle. We knew that God had told us to stay with the Suruwahá, that we were their family. This was the only thing we were sure of, and it was another reason that Suzuki decided to move into the Casai with them.

As the days slowly went by, the Suruwahá were getting more and more agitated in the Casai. One morning Naru hit his son. This is unheard of among the Suruwahá; they are never violent toward their children. He then took a machete and cut his hammock down the middle. Kusiuma did the same to hers. We were really worried because cutting their hammock is usually the last thing the Suruwahá do before committing suicide.

Immediately Suzuki informed the authorities that the Indians were going to commit suicide if they didn't do something. It would have looked really bad for the authorities if the Suruwahá were to die in the Casai. Officials arranged for a plane to take them home the next morning. But Tititu would need to repeat medical tests every six months, and Iganani needed more treatment.

Suzuki and I reacted by sending informative e-mails to everyone we knew. We contacted all the authorities and again explained the situation.

It worked, and a meeting was called with the Suruwahá in a couple of days to discuss the situation. It was a temporary victory. We were going to be the translators in the meeting. We asked everyone we knew to pray.

The meeting was held in the Casai. A room was filled with twenty professionals invited by the Coordinator for Indigenous Health in the state of Amazonas, including doctors, anthropologists, a federal prosecutor, representatives from CIMI (Catholic missionaries for Indians), and even one agent from ABIN, the national intelligence agency, who had been sent by Brazil's national president.

The federal prosecutor was leading the meeting. He questioned Muwaji first, spending the whole time trying to show that Muwaji wanted to kill her daughter. He tried to prove we were the ones who had forced her to come and save Iganani.

"Do you like your daughter?" he asked Muwaji. "Are you sure you don't want to kill her as is normal in your culture? Are you sure you want treatment? If you want to go home, that means you don't want treatment." Muwaji was getting more and more confused and frustrated.

"You know she will never be normal, never walk or talk," he went on.

The questions continued and the meeting went on for four hours, but I was so impressed with Naru again. He addressed the federal prosecutor, asking his name, and then spoke directly to him.

"Next time you hear there are Suruwahá in your city, stay in your house, don't bother to come out. We have nothing to do with you. You are not our family," he said, eyes burning. "Have you ever killed a jaguar?" he asked.

The federal prosecutor shook his head.

"Have you ever killed a tapir?" Naru went on.

Again he shook his head.

"So you know nothing. How can we listen to you?"

Despite Naru's speech, after four hours of questioning the Suruwahá were humiliated. Muwaji had had enough, so frustrated by the questions.

"Okay, fine, I will go home and kill my daughter," she said, defeated.

I hated to translate her words, but I had to.

As I told them what she had said, immediately the federal prosecutor and indigenous health department official left the room. Half an hour later they returned, looking pleased with themselves.

"We, the representatives of the government of Brazil, concerned with the welfare of the Indians, have decided to send these families back to their village. Everyone here heard what Muwaji said. She wants to go back, and we must honor her wishes and respect her culture," the prosecutor said.

We were all shocked. Two of the nurses walked out of the room crying.

At this point *I* had had enough. Usually I never raise my voice, but I could not contain my frustration.

"You are being irresponsible!" I shouted, looking straight into the eyes of the prosecutor; my whole body was shaking with feeling at what I was saying.

Suzuki and the Indians were looking at me in shock, my outburst was so uncharacteristic. But I couldn't stop now.

"If you make them go back, you will be responsible for their deaths, because they will kill their children and then they will kill themselves," I continued.

The prosecutor was a big man, but as I said that, his disposition changed and his shoulders slumped, as if I had taken the wind out of him.

"Well, what shall I do?" he asked feebly.

"I don't know. You have convinced them to go home now," I said furiously.

Once the Suruwahá have set their minds on something, they are very hard to dissuade. I didn't know if we had any hope.

One of the anthropologists spoke up, saying the meeting had gone on for too long, and it was obvious the Suruwahá loved their children. Eventually it was decided that the plane would leave the next day from Manaus to Lábrea, where there would be a boat waiting to take the Indians the rest of the way home. If I could convince Muwaji not to go back and kill Iganani when we got to Lábrea, I could bring them back to Manaus and her situation would be reconsidered.

That evening we got home and sent out hundreds of e-mails requesting prayer. I knew the lives of the Indians were balancing on the brink and that we needed to pray for a breakthrough.

The next morning we flew to Lábrea. Muwaji and Iganani were both crying the whole way. Iganani had been in the meeting where Muwaji had said she would bury her. As she said that, Iganani let out a wail of terror. She was nearly two years old and understood everything that was going on.

As we landed in Lábrea, there was a car waiting to take them to the boat. I had to explain what was happening. As Muwaji got into the car, she suddenly gave Iganani to me.

"Márcia, she is yours. I can't kill her," she said through her tears before getting in the car.

Another YWAMer called Darcy, who also spoke Suruwahá, went with the Indians to the boat, and I took Iganani and Hakani to the YWAM base in Lábrea. Iganani was inconsolable. I had to go out and buy some baby food, but nothing would placate her. She was screaming for her mother.

But Muwaji was just as upset. The boat was supposed to leave at 2:00 p.m. and was going to take five days, but because of the state Muwaji was in, they could not leave. She was so desperate. Soon the whole town heard of the wailing Indian on the boat. Darcy came to me in tears; he had been with Muwaji for hours.

"You can't take Iganani. Muwaji will kill herself," he said.

I felt this was a test and I had to stand firm. I loved Muwaji but knew she had given me her daughter because she didn't want to kill her. If I gave her back, Muwaji would feel she had no choice but to go through with it. I decided not to talk to Muwaji, because I knew if I saw her crying, I would waver in my decision.

The boat still hadn't left and it was early evening. Suzuki and I were trying to calm Iganani, and Darcy was with Muwaji.

It just so happened that next door to the YWAM base where we were staying lived the mother of a man named Isaac who was the head of FUNAI in Lábrea. She had heard Iganani crying for hours, and like everyone else in the city, knew that Iganani's mother was crying on the boat.

Suzuki had been over to talk to Isaac. He said I should try and speak to him as well. I didn't know what Suzuki had said, but I knew that this FUNAI official was a compassionate man. He was the one who had given us the license to go to São Paulo in the first place.

When I knocked on the door, I found the official in the middle of a gaggle of elderly women with his head in his hands. They were all telling him that as the leader of FUNAI he had to do something. His mother and her friends were telling him to sort out the problem with Muwaji and Iganani.

"Okay, let's go and talk to Muwaji," he finally said, exasperated by the nagging.

I took him to the boat, where we found Muwaji with a swollen face and puffy eyes from all her crying. I could see she was suffering so much. Everything in me was holding back the tears that I wanted to weep for her.

"Muwaji, you gave me Iganani, and I am not going to give her back to you. But you can come back to Manaus with us," I said with the FUNAI official as a witness.

Muwaji agreed. I couldn't believe it and breathed a sigh of relief. Naru's family left on the boat the next day, and we spent the night talking to authorities in Manaus by telephone, telling them what had happened and that Muwaji was coming back. The coordinator of FUNASA had agreed that Muwaji and Iganani would stay only one night in Manaus, and then we would go to Brasília. The Suruwahá could stay in a hotel and wouldn't have to go back to the Indian House. This was Muwaji's main fear; she hated the place with a passion. I explained to her she would not have to stay there again, so she agreed to come.

On the plane to Manaus, the Suruwahá were crying. I could see Muwaji felt responsible for the situation they were in and was trying to be strong. Her brother Aji was irritated with her for crying. He blamed her tears for taking them back to Manaus.

Suzuki was put in another plane to travel to Manaus, and I was with Muwaji and her family in a five-passenger plane. We arrived first and were met by the coordinator for health in the Amazon. He was a big man and very angry. He didn't like Indians.

"Muwaji is going with her family to the Indian House," he said as soon as he saw us.

"But when I talked to you last night, you said she would only have to stay in Manaus one night, and they could go to a hotel. She is very traumatized and can't go to the Indian House," I replied.

But he was adamant. He said he was representing the state; they are responsible for the Indians, and it was not my place to interfere. He then said the Suruwahá no longer had the right to an interpreter, and I couldn't go with them. Moreover, if we didn't agree, they would be sent straight back to the tribe. My heart sank, knowing how Muwaji would react when I told her she had to go to the Indian House.

I tried to suggest that I would pay for her hotel, and the government wouldn't have to pay, but the coordinator wasn't having any of it. We were recording the conversation in case we needed it as evidence. The coordinator was saying I would be sued if I paid for her medical treatment and sued if I did anything to interfere.

I was crying as I went to talk to Muwaji, knowing that she and her family wouldn't stay but would go home and kill themselves. Silently I prayed under my breath, beseeching God to intervene.

I told Muwaji what was happening and asked what she wanted to do.

"I am going back. I can't stay there," she said, crying.

Adilson, the manager from the Indian House, had arrived and was standing in the background. He went over to Muwaji and, with tears in his eyes, knelt down and begged her not to go back. She had no idea what he was saying in Portuguese, but she was obviously touched by his emotion.

He was telling her not to be afraid, that it would only be one night, and he would make sure they were all safe.

I translated what he was saying, and to my amazement, Muwaji said she would go with him.

By the time Suzuki arrived in the second plane, Muwaji was already on her way. He raced over to join the Suruwahá in the Indian House, but when he arrived he was denied entrance, even though he had just been living there for a month. He waited outside so the Suruwahá could see him by the fence and know he was there.

I was desperately trying to find out what was happening. Eventually we heard that the Suruwahá were going to be sent to Brasília in four days. By now the story was in all the newspapers. I flew down to Brasília with Hakani to meet Muwaji, her brother, and Iganani. Suzuki stayed in Manaus to make sure they were put on the plane.

He called to tell me what time they were landing. A Christian woman named Dr. Damares Alves had called the television station and arranged for them to be with me at the airport.

Damares, a parliamentary assessor, became a very close friend and helped us on numerous occasions. She worked for a government minister, Deputy Henrique Afonso. As a lawyer, she had always been interested in indigenous issues, especially infanticide. Damares had prayed for years that God would show her someone to help bring the issue to Congress. She felt she had no legitimacy to talk about infanticide, as she had never worked directly with Indians. When she saw us on the *Fantástico* TV show back in 2005, Damares immediately knew that we were the right people for this fight. Infanticide was only one of Damares's battles; she was defending the rights of children in every area of Brazil.

"I'm here," I shouted and waved when I saw Muwaji coming through the doors. Immediately she was whisked away by guards—they wouldn't let me near her. The national media filmed how I, the only interpreter, was being kept away from the Suruwahá.

Suzuki arrived the next day, and with Damares and the television crew, we went to the Indian House to ask to see Muwaji.

Because we were there with the media and Damares, we were let in. Muwaji was filmed saying she loved her daughter but could not live in the Indian House.

After her interview was aired, the authorities were given twenty-four hours to find the Suruwahá an interpreter. Obviously Suzuki and I were the only choice, so Suzuki moved into the Indian House with Muwaji and her brother, and I rented an apartment close by with Hakani.

Muwaji, her children, and her brother ended up being in the Indian House for two months as Iganani received treatment at the hospital.

Dr. Maíra Barreto, a lawyer, and Dr. Keila Pinezi, a Christian anthropologist and journalist, joined Damares in our fight. They advised us to start a nonprofit organization. So in September we founded Atini— Voice for Life—located in Brasília, to defend the rights of indigenous children. Atini means "voice" in the Suruwahá language. God would help us make that voice loud and clear.

SEVENTEEN

An Uphill Battle

IT WAS AN UPHILL BATTLE trying to keep Muwaji and her family in the Indian House in Brasília for three months. Every day she wanted to leave. There were about one hundred and fifty Indians in the building, it was full of disease, the mattresses were dirty, and it was infested with mosquitoes.

We were trying everything we could to get Muwaji's family out, contacting lawyers and government officials we knew, but nothing seemed to work. In the middle of it all, Suzuki and I were again invited to go to Norway for two months to teach at a linguistics school. It was a hard decision to make. How could we leave Muwaji in the middle of everything? In the end, we felt it was right to go.

Hakani needed a new passport, and it was uncertain whether they would issue it in time, but after much prayer we finally had the passport in our hands on the day we were to fly. Darcy and his family moved in with Muwaji to help look after her.

We realized as soon as we left the country that the trip was a gift from God. It gave us the refreshing we needed in the middle of the battle. It also gave us perspective. We suddenly realized how ridiculous the situation was. We had been fighting, asking for permission for Muwaji to leave the Indian House, but as we talked to people in Norway about the situation, we realized Muwaji and the other Indians were free. They didn't have to stay in the house if they didn't want to. They were not prisoners.

We spoke to Muwaji and Aji from Norway on Skype, translating the text of the United Nations declaration that says "everyone has the right to freedom of movement and residence." We explained they were not children and did not have to stay where they did not want to. I wasn't sure they understood, but the next morning when Darcy called us, I realized they had.

Muwaji had packed all their things and walked out of the house.

"We are not children. We don't have to stay," she said as she walked down the street.

The Indian House is far from anywhere. It could be dangerous for them to be walking by themselves, so Darcy rushed to get a car and picked them up to take them to the apartment where his wife was staying.

There was pandemonium in the Indian House when the government officials found out the Suruwahá had left. As soon as Muwaji arrived at his apartment, Darcy contacted the authorities to let them know what had happened. He then called us, and we all started praying for the Suruwahá. It felt as if the spiritual warfare had just heated up.

Again, officials claimed we had kidnapped the Suruwahá and would have to give them back or face being arrested and going to prison. As we prayed, we felt we were either on the side of the Suruwahá or on the side of the government. It was all or nothing. We knew the Universal Declaration of Human Rights says the Indians are free. God says they are free. Therefore, it was their decision if they wanted to go back or not.

Darcy asked Muwaji and Aji if they wanted to go back. The answer was an emphatic no. We knew we had to support them and not give in to intimidation, but it was tough. The federal police were sent to the apartment to take the Indians by force. Damares knew it was happening, so before they could get there she sent an official car to pick up the Suruwahá and have them taken to the nation's congressional building where they couldn't be arrested.

By this time Suzuki and I had returned from Norway. We decided to rent a bigger house for everyone to live in. The police hadn't returned since Damares had intervened, and it seemed we and the Suruwahá had succeeded.

From July 2006 to January 2007 we lived in the new rented house with everyone. Muwaji loved it. Iganani was getting her treatment; all was well at last. But then the authorities sent a team to the house to try and convince Muwaji and her family to go back to the Indian House. They were very intimidating and tried to make us convince the Suruwahá to go back. We agreed to translate for them, but we were not going to convince the Suruwahá to do anything they did not want to do. An official meeting was called with an anthropologist who wanted to talk to the Suruwahá. Suzuki arranged for a friend to videotape everything, because we were frightened they might try to take the Indians by force.

We met at our house. The officials had brought a van with them, hoping to take the Suruwahá back with them. Before anyone had a chance to say anything, Aji started talking. Everyone was sitting round the table, and he pointed to each one of them, saying:

"Listen to me. I see your eyes. I see you are angry. I know you don't like me or my friends. But do you know my name?"

The men fumbled with their paperwork, unable to look Aji in the eye. He was completely in control, talking from his heart.

"Have you killed a jaguar?" he asked.

Each man shook his head.

"Have you walked in the jungle and killed a snake?" Aji went on.

Again the men shook their heads.

Finally Aji told them that he was not going back to the Indian House, that he wanted to stay with us. Then he looked at each man and asked them if they understood what he was saying.

Each man nodded his head, shocked by the force and authority of what Aji was saying. I was so impressed. The men talked among themselves and then left. There was nothing they could say. We sent a letter to the authorities again, explaining the outcome; we had learned from the lawyer that it was important that everyone knew the details of what had happened. Everything was filmed and well documented.

After the men left, we didn't hear any more from the authorities. The Suruwahá stayed in the house with us, and in January 2007 they went back to the tribe. The doctors said it was important for them to go back awhile, but Iganani would need to return to the city for more treatment.

During this time Damares's boss, Deputy Henrique Afonso, decided he was going to leave politics. He was a Christian from the north of Brazil and had become very disillusioned with politics. He felt it was impossible to do anything worthwhile amid such corruption. One evening he and his wife prayed and asked God for a sign as to whether he should stay in politics or not. The next day I had been given five minutes to speak in Congress. Henrique Afonso was there as I spoke. As it was such a short time, I projected an image of Iganani and told Muwaji's story, explaining the situation and why we needed the government's help.

When Henrique saw Iganani's face, he felt God speak to him, telling him to stay in politics because He still had work for him there. Henrique was very popular with the people because of his reputation for honesty and integrity. He was reelected into the ruling party and dedicated his service to the lives of Indian children and eradicating infanticide. God was raising up people of power and influence to help Iganani and the many others who would follow her.

On Mother's Day 2007 Henrique organized a celebration in Congress to honor mothers. He had chosen four women to honor. One was Kamiru, a woman from the Xingu tribe who had saved Amalé, the son of a neighbor, from being abandoned. He was buried alive and Kamiru had to dig him out of the grave. Suzuki had met Kamiru when he stayed in the Casai for three months helping Muwaji and Iganani. She had shown Amalé to Suzuki and told the story of saving his life. Suzuki told me about Kamiru. I went to meet her, and over time we developed a friendship. Later, when a friend suggested to her that she live with us, Suzuki and I agreed, as she had nowhere comfortable to stay while taking Amalé to the hospital.

Henrique Afonso also honored me in the celebration. That same day he was planning to launch a bill to stop infanticide. It was to be called Muwaji's Bill. But the problem was that he could not write the bill by himself. He would need others, including a team of lawyers, to draw it up. Five days before the Mother's Day celebration, he called Suzuki and me.

"Do you think you can help us to write a bill in five days?" he asked.

I laughed; I didn't think I could write a bill in five years. But as he asked me, I knew it was from the Lord and that somehow He would help us, so I agreed.

"Great, if you can have it ready by the morning of May 11, I will announce it as an official bill," he said.

Then started the most hectic five days of our lives. We hardly slept but contacted all the lawyers we knew to enlist their help.

Previously, if a person knew a child was in danger of being abandoned, it was illegal to interfere. Tribal customs, good or bad, had to be protected. We wanted to make it law for anyone who was aware of a child in danger to notify the authorities. We gave a few instructions on how this could be done in a culturally acceptable way.

Finally, by 9:00 a.m. on May 11, 2007, Muwaji's Bill was finished. We were all exhausted but jubilant that the work was done. There were still lots of spelling errors, but we had no time to change things. We had to send it to Damares, who would read and approve it before having it officially stamped as a bill.

We e-mailed the twelve pages through, and Damares printed them out on official paper. She then ran downstairs to register the bill and hand it to Henrique, who was waiting to take it to the nation. It was a race against time, as Henrique was about to start his speech any minute but was holding off, waiting for the bill. Each week a member of Congress gave a speech on national television, chosen by lottery. It just so happened that on that day Henrique had been picked to speak.

Just before Henrique went on the air, Damares flung the bill into his hands. She quickly called and told us to turn on the TV so we could hear his message, which was being broadcast live. We were all cheering and screaming as we heard him talking about the right to life, holding the bill that we had finished only an hour earlier. Until that moment, we had felt that what we were trying to do was impossible. As we saw Muwaji's Bill being aired to the whole nation, we knew that God was in this. He had made it happen.

Henrique then went to speak to Congress about the bill. As he spoke, the anointing of God fell on him. Usually all the politicians are talking among themselves, but as Henrique spoke, they all stopped what they were doing to listen to him. He explained that the bill's name was in honor of Muwaji and her fight to save Iganani.

After he had spoken, we had a huge celebration outside the congress building. We released five hundred helium balloons into the air as a prophetic act. Each balloon represented one of five hundred children killed. We attached crosses to the balloons and had one minute of silence for those who had died.

It had all happened so fast, but we knew it was only the beginning. God had shown He was with us; we had seen His power guiding and directing us. Now we had to continue to stand and be a voice for those who had no voice.

EIGHTEEN

A Voice for the Voiceless

DESPITE THE VICTORIES, we were still facing persecution. As a mission we were often misunderstood by other missionary organizations, and it was hard to achieve unity. Our national TV coverage on *Fantástico* had made things harder for other missions, who all had to re-register and fill out complicated documents for the government. Our heart was always for unity, and we were troubled that we had caused problems for others.

Suzuki and I decided to write an open letter to all the other missions working with Indians. We apologized that they had been affected by what had happened to us. We explained that we felt we had to be faithful to the gospel we preached and continue fighting to stop infanticide.

God had clearly spoken to us through Proverbs 31:8, which in the New King James translation says: "Open your mouth for the speechless, in the cause of all who are appointed to die."

We had to open our mouths for the children who were appointed to die and fight for them. We knew we had to speak out and make a noise. God had said that He would put us in the spotlight, but we were to use the visibility to speak for the voiceless children, never for our own rights as missionaries.

As a result of the spotlight, which brought its own pressures of constant attack and persecution, we were becoming well known. Others who were fighting to save children contacted us. Through the Atini organization we were able to give them advice and access to lawyers and anthropologists who could help them.

The result of the letter was so positive, we had unanimous support. One large mission that had distanced itself from YWAM in the past embraced us. They invited Suzuki and me to come and speak at the church where the head of the mission was the pastor. The congregation was so touched by our story, and the pastor publically stood with us, declaring his support.

God was using our persecution to unite His body. I was also invited to speak about infanticide at the National Congress for Missionaries held in the city of Águas de Lindóia, in the state of São Paulo. I had never heard of a YWAMer being asked to give an address to the whole crowd on the closing evening.

As God told us to open our mouths and make a noise about the issue of infanticide, we had it in our hearts to film a documentary. But we had no expertise to do it ourselves.

In December 2007 I was in Kona, Hawaii, with Suzuki and Hakani, doing linguistics work for YWAM. We were working on Uniskript, which is a scientific methodology that can be applied to any language to generate alphabets, enabling people to learn to read and write within days or even hours. It was an exciting project to be part of, but I hoped being in Kona would help us with leads for the film as well.

I knew that David Cunningham, the son of YWAM founder Loren Cunningham, was a Hollywood director, and I thought he would be perfect to make a film. But everyone I asked told me it would never work, that he was much too busy. Discouraged, I gave up trying to meet him.

On the day we were leaving to return to Brazil, we were having lunch at a friend's house when David happened to drop by with his children. He had heard of Hakani's story, and his children had been praying for her so they wanted to meet her.

In her usual gregarious way, Hakani welcomed the family with open arms, sharing her cookies and sweets with the children. As they were playing, I knew it was my only chance to talk to David.

"Would you come to Brazil to make a documentary about infanticide in the tribes?" I asked outright.

David asked a few questions about the story and how graphic the film could be.

"It would have to be very graphic," I replied. We wanted to be able to show it to the Indians so they would see and understand.

He said he thought that we should pray right there and then about whether it was right for him to make the movie or not. The three of us bowed our heads in prayer. After a few minutes David looked up, and I knew he had an answer.

"I feel like we have to make this film, and soon. I sense an urgency," he told me.

Suzuki and I couldn't have been happier. We tried to extend our ticket home to discuss the documentary more, but frustratingly it was impossible. So we flew home that evening.

We had only just landed in Brazil when we got an e-mail message from David saying the crew was ready and would arrive in the next couple of weeks to make the film. We were astounded. There was a strike in Hollywood at the time, so he had been able to get many people to come out. Some were paid, but others volunteered simply because they were touched by the story.

Everything seemed to be going according to plan, except for one thing. I got sick. On the flight home from Hawaii, the left side of my face and jaw started to ache. By the time we landed in Rio, I was in intense pain and had to go straight to the hospital.

"You have an infection between the bone and flesh in your head. It is very serious," the doctor said.

They didn't know where it had come from, how I had contracted it, or whether it was meningitis or something different. I stayed in the hospital for three days on an IV and then went to my parents' with Hakani. Suzuki had to go on to Brasília to make arrangements for the film.

I was feeling terrible, but I knew I had to get better, as they needed me for the film. Suzuki and I were the only Suruwahá interpreters who spoke English. When David heard that I might not be able to be there, he said they couldn't make the documentary without me. I was desperate. I asked the doctor if I could fly, and he said there was no way. The infection was so bad that the air pressure on the plane could prove fatal. Two other doctors confirmed his prognosis. I wasn't even allowed to travel by bus because I would go via Brasília, and the high altitude could worsen the infection, which could damage my brain.

All I could do was rest at home. I was so sick that pus was trickling down my nose and out of my eyes. Later the doctors said I was lucky not to have gone blind. After being at home for nearly three weeks, I wasn't getting any better. I had scans of my head that showed the infection still covering the same area. The antibiotics didn't seem to be reducing it at all. I was feeling worse than ever, but I was still asking God if I could go.

Suzuki, still in Brasília, had forwarded me an e-mail from Francisca Irving, a missionary from the Porto Velho base. Francisca quoted Exodus 14:15–16 about God telling Moses to stretch out his staff to part the sea so the Israelites could cross over. She said that when I touched the airplane to travel to the Amazon, I would be well. As I read the e-mail, I had a gift of faith and I knew I should go. My sister Maryangela, who before had been adamant that I stay at home, read the e-mail and said, "Yes, I think you should go."

So after Suzuki prayed for me over the phone, arrangements were made for me to fly to Porto Velho, where the movie was being filmed. At home I was so sick I could barely stand, but I made it to the plane. My friend who sent the e-mail was right—as soon as I got on the plane I started to feel better. When I arrived in Porto Velho, I miraculously felt fine.

For the next two weeks of filming I was on my feet all hours of the day, running to and fro. I was completely well, despite the exhausting timetable and the intense heat of the jungle. Later I went to a doctor in Porto Velho. He scanned my head again and said it looked like the infection was still there, but what he saw could be scarring instead of actual infection.

When I first became ill, Suzuki shared about my sickness in a church in Brasília. Later a woman came up to him. She was a Christian and in government. She had had a vision of me before she knew I was ill, with a gun pointed to the left side of my head and my cheek peppered with pellets. She had recently been talking to someone in authority about me. The man looked at a picture of me and said, "That lady is going to die before the end of the year." I got sick on the last day of the year. But I did not die. We knew then that it was a spiritual attack against my life, but God cannot be stopped, and I came through.

Helping with the documentary was such a wonderful experience. It was to be called *Hakani*, as the issue of infanticide was being told through her story. The whole YWAM base in Porto Velho took part in some way. David Cunningham wanted Indians who were involved in saving children to be in the film. The crew filmed the burial scene over several days, making it like a game for the children. They used chocolate cake instead of mud, and jelly candy for the worms that the child playing Hakani had to eat. The boy who played Hakani's brother was so touched by the experience. He said God had told him in a dream to take part in the film. He is now working with rescued children as a missionary himself.

It was all finished by February 2008 and then took about another month to edit. We were concerned about how Hakani would react to seeing a film about her life, but she was overjoyed. She loves the Suruwahá and beams with pride when she sees her people on film.

Seeing the movie being made was a very special time for Hakani, as she was reunited with her brother Bibi, who happened to be in Porto Velho. Hakani was so excited to see him. The Suruwahá don't hug, and so Bibi didn't quite know how to react to his little sister flinging her arms around him. It was so touching to see his amazement as he looked at his sister, who had grown into such a strong, healthy, loving girl. Hakani gave her brother gifts of chocolate and a flashlight, which he shyly accepted with a big smile.

In April 2008 David Cunningham took the finished documentary to an official screening at the State Department and Congress in Washington, D.C. I then went to New York with Hakani and our Atini lawyer, Maíra Barreto, to a conference about indigenous Indians around the world at the United Nations. The film was shown to one of the eight delegates who work for indigenous Indians. He was very moved and gave us advice on how to go forward.

After two weeks we returned to Brazil, where the documentary had made the national press. Some government officials were not pleased with it and started a campaign against the film, saying that it should be banned, it had offended the Indians, and that everyone involved in the film would be sued.

What they did not realize was that any publicity, however bad, was still publicity. Because people were talking about the film, more people got to see it, curious as to what the fuss was about.

The *Hakani* film was to do more good than we could have imagined. It helped bring global attention to the issue of infanticide in the Amazon Basin and launch a national movement for the approval of a law to protect indigenous families. In August 2008 there was a public hearing in Congress for Muwaji's Bill. It had been with a deputy for over a year, waiting for her report on the bill before it could be passed as a new law. After her report it then had to be voted on in the Human Rights Committee, and then all the deputies would vote on it. She hadn't produced a report and was stalling, using delay tactics so that the bill wouldn't get passed.

Enock Freire, a Brazilian friend, knew we had to do something to get the bill through. He organized demonstrations in fourteen cities in Brazil, protesting infanticide and raising awareness of the bill. The newspapers were talking about "the population of Brazil taking to the streets to defend the rights of indigenous children." We turned up at a public meeting of Congress with many of the children whose lives had been saved. Each of the children handed the deputies Indian dolls.

The president of the committee was a man named Pompeo de Mattos. He had seen the *Hakani* film and had been very touched by it. He told the committee it was not possible for anyone to say it was normal to bury a child alive. A young Indian man then came to speak to the committee. Matasempe Mayoruna was from an isolated tribe. He had been born a twin, but his father had not wanted to kill his two sons as was expected. When the children were ten, a shaman-chief from another village came to the tribe and found out the twins had lived.

"They must die. You must kill them now," he said.

"Is there any way I can die in their place?" the father pleaded in desperation.

The witch doctor relented and allowed him to die in the place of one of his sons. In horror, Matasempe watched his brother and father tied together and burned alive. The traumatized Matasempe was later saved by a military man and taken to live in Rio. He told the committee that they must help stop the tradition. The reason he was speaking up was because he had seen the *Hakani* film. He had never talked about what had happened to his father and brother, but now he felt it was time to speak out.

Pompeo de Mattos summed up the meeting by saying Hakani and Matasempe were symbols of the fight and that the deputies must listen to what the Indians were saying. He arranged a public hearing to watch the documentary in November 2008.

The very next day the deputy who had been stalling gave her report to pass Muwaji's Bill. She had changed some of the text, removing many of the government's obligations, but we were still encouraged at the impact we had made. Unknown to us at the time, Pompeo de Mattos was able to propose an amendment to the Constitution of Brazil, which is not an easy thing to do. The signatures of over a third of the members of Congress are needed. Pompeo's proposed amendment stated that the right to life was higher than the Indians' right to keep their culture.

This was of far greater significance than Muwaji's Bill, because it meant infanticide would not be condoned by the government any more. We were amazed that after the battle to get Muwaji's Bill through, he had been able to slip the proposal in, although the process for the constitution to be amended takes many years.

Muwaji's Law (officially called Law Project 1057) was eventually approved at the Congressional Committee of Human Rights and Minorities in June 2011. At this writing, it is now going to the Committee of Constitution and Justice, which defines where in the Brazilian law system it will be placed. Then it goes to the plenary session of Congress and the Senate for formal approval and is signed by the president of Brazil.

Miguel Martins, a Catholic deputy, saw the *Hakani* documentary and as a result made an amendment in the Adoption Law, which was going through its final stages. He inserted that "indigenous children at risk of being murdered due to cultural reasons should be put up for adoption, preferably within the tribe, but if that is not possible, anywhere else."

Damares called me excitedly when this happened, saying it was being transmitted live on television. I was not at home, so I quickly called my mother in Rio and asked her to turn on the TV. Sure enough, she saw Miguel talking about the documentary and the issue of infanticide. The amendment was passed unanimously in the Congress.

ONE OF THE INDIANS who had been working on the *Hakani* film was a man named Paje Kajabi. He had been a chief in the Xingu tribe and now worked for FUNAI. He and his wife had saved a little girl from being buried alive and then adopted her. They had also adopted twins, rescuing them from death. I had gotten to know them in Brasília and had become friends with Paje's wife, Diva. She dreamed, like me, of being able to help all the rejected children. Paje and Diva felt encouraged by us, knowing we were fighting with them for the same outcome.

They had started their own nongovernmental organization (NGO), similar to Atini but directed entirely by the Indians. Paje loved the *Hakani* film so much he wanted to show it to all the Indians in Xingu Park, a reservation for indigenous tribes.

We had first been invited to Xingu Park in 2007 by Kamiru's brother Paltu. He had heard that we were helping Kamiru and Amalé and was deeply touched. His wife had birthed twins, and they had been forced to kill one of the babies. Paltu was one of the leaders of the reservation, which had been created by the government in 1961 to protect the Indians. Fourteen different tribes were living in the park. It was a beautiful place with no mosquitoes.

Missionaries had never been allowed into Xingu Park. Indians had been told that missionaries were dangerous and would try to steal their culture. However, Paltu made an official invitation for us to come to the annual *kuarup* ritual. The ritual is an important ceremony to honor the lives of whoever has died that year. The Indians sing songs about the hope of resurrection. They believe they used to have the power of resurrection but lost it because of their sin.

Many of the Indians in the Xingu tribe are educated. Paltu himself was an academic and had written articles about his language. He was proud of his culture and would still paint himself even while living in Brasília.

We stayed in Xingu Park for three weeks. We went on fishing expeditions and camped by a tranquil lake. Every morning I would wake up overcome with emotion, and tears would prick my eyes as I realized we were actually in Xingu Park, a place we thought we could never go.

While there, I was taken into the home of one of the chiefs. It was a large hut covered with thatch. In the corner there was an area closed off with cloth and thatch. It was very dark. I was slowly taken closer in and suddenly realized there was a young girl living in the dark. She was kept in a hammock and not allowed to leave her hiding place. Her name was Kanhu Raka and she was nine years old. Her family loved her but realized she had a disability, so they hid her from the rest of the tribe. She was not getting any medical treatment.

I told the family to take her to the hospital in Brasília. They agreed, and she was diagnosed with muscular dystrophy. The doctors told her father there was no cure and she must return to the tribe. Kanhu was desperate; she didn't want to live the rest of her days hidden in the dark.

I rushed to the hospital after her father called to explain what was going on, but when I arrived the social worker said I was not allowed to speak to the doctors. She said there was nothing they could do for Kanhu and she should be taken back to the tribe. Frustrated, I went home and researched muscular dystrophy on the Internet. A place in São Paulo called the Genoma Institute treated the disease. I called them and explained the problem. They said they could help Kanhu and told us to bring her to them.

Suzuki flew with the family to the Institute. The doctors were very friendly, but at the first consultation an anthropologist was present. He said the treatment could not go ahead until they had the approval of the whole tribe. The family looked to Suzuki in desperation. They had come all this way and now were being refused treatment. However, some of the other doctors had mercy and decided to go ahead anyway. They gave Kanhu tablets and physiotherapy as well as putting braces on her legs to straighten them out. A church in São Paulo gave her a wheelchair, and her life was transformed.

Kanhu's situation was not unusual. We knew there were many other children with disabilities who hadn't been killed but were kept hidden.

A year after our trip to Xingu Park, Paje was planning to organize the meeting for all the Indians in the park to watch the *Hakani* film. It was no small task. Paje's NGO sent an official request to Atini for help, and Enock traveled to Xingu Park to document the three days of meetings. Indians came in from all over the area, many coming by boat or walking through the jungle.

We didn't know how the Indians would take the film. The government had said they would be offended, but the truth was they loved it so much they wanted it played before every meeting. Paje had only planned to show it once. After each showing many Indians would come and share their stories. One said he was a survivor of infanticide. His mother had tried to kill him because he was born on a lunar eclipse, but his grandmother rescued him. Another young man said, "My heart cries when I think of all the children under the ground. I want to see children above the ground playing. Please stop burying your children."

At the end of the three days, Aritana Yawalapiti, the chief of Xingu Park, summarized their experience.

"We have met many times to discuss the land or gold miners," he said. "But we have never talked about our children. Now it is time to talk about our children."

He started by making a promise to stop burying twins and children born to single mothers. But he was honest and said they would need help with disabled children.

One by one, seven chiefs came up and made a solemn promise to do all they could to stop their people from killing babies.

They asked us to provide a place for their disabled children so they wouldn't have to be killed. It was a historic event, and when Suzuki and I heard what had happened, we could not contain our emotion. We hoped one day all the tribes in the Amazon would follow the example of those in Xingu Park, and countless children's lives would be saved.

Epilogue: Home

IN THE MIDST of everything happening around us, I remembered that day at the Palavra da Vida church camp when I was eleven years old. I recalled throwing my stick into the roaring fire to answer the missionary call. I had felt then that God was asking if I was willing to follow the way He had designed for me, even though I didn't know where it would lead. As I walked toward the bonfire, I said yes in my heart and immediately felt such a sense of peace. Now, over thirty years later, I was amazed at what God had done. He used me, a simple Brazilian girl, just as he had used a Suruwahá widow, the least in one of the smallest Amazonian tribes, to work His purposes out. All He needed was a willing and obedient heart, and He did the rest.

At this time we were praying for a safe place for the increasing number of Indians who were coming to us for refuge. Our small apartment in Brasília was full to bursting, so we had had to rent other buildings around the city to accommodate the families. Our desire was to have a farm where the Indians could live as they do in the jungle, but it seemed an almost impossible dream. However, in faith we started looking at properties and found one just outside Brasília that might work. The only problem was that it cost $400,000 and we didn't have any money.

In early 2009 we were all back in Kona to continue our work on Uniskript. There were many Discipleship Training Schools running at the time, and we were asked to share about our work with the All Nations All Generations DTS. Suzuki and I spoke about our ministry with the Suruwahá and all that was happening, and then Ieru Toomoa, one of the leaders, asked if we had any prayer requests. I immediately thought of the property and so mentioned we were planning to buy land for the Indian families. The whole school of about one hundred people prayed for us, and we were so grateful. At the end one of the students from England came up to ask me more details. He asked about the property and how much it would cost. When I told him the details, he said he might be able to help. I thought perhaps he would be giving $100, and that would be wonderful—the first offering toward the property. However, he came back and told us he would be able to give almost the entire amount. We were astounded and praised the Lord for His provision.

On returning to Brazil we pursued purchasing the property, but when we were going to sign for it, we found the previous owners had no deeds for the land, so the sale fell through. We were disappointed, but I had a sense God was going to give us something even better.

Within a few days we heard about a farm half an hour outside Brasília. It had ninety-six acres of land and was owned by an old woman who had turned it into a model farm. Even her garden had been designed by a famous landscape architect!

When Suzuki and I went to look around, we knew it would be perfect. It was filled with animals—chickens, pigs, even peacocks. There was a swimming pool, a main house, and room to build a school for the children and more accommodation for the families. The sale took about a year to complete, and I cried tears of joy when we eventually moved into *Casa das Nações* (House of the Nations) with sixty Indians from different tribes in December 2010.

Because of the *Hakani* documentary, we were now well known among the Indians, and we were able to welcome a family right away who had given birth to twins. One of the twins had been killed, and the couple had fled their tribe to avoid the surviving twin being buried alive as well.

A year before we moved onto the farm, a beautiful event took place in my family. My niece, Sarah, got married to Kakatsa, an Indian from the Kamaiurá tribe. Sarah had been adopted when she was a baby by my sister Margaret. Her story is a miracle, as she had been born at six months weighing only a little over two pounds. Margaret's gynecologist called, asking if Margaret wanted to adopt a little girl who had been abandoned by her mother, even though she might not live long.

Margaret made her way to the doctor immediately, and when she held Sarah in her arms, it was love at first sight. The doctor gave her some medicine to help her lungs and told my sister that Sarah was a miracle child. Even though she was tiny, she was fully formed and developed and had no defects from her premature birth. She could not suck at first, so my sister had to put cotton wool soaked with milk near her mouth so she could take it in. Sarah had to have a hot water bottle close to her at all times to keep her tiny body warm. Through much prayer and love, Sarah grew up into a beautiful young woman.

She was living with us in Brasília when she met Kakatsa. They were the same age and had similar stories, both having been rejected at birth. Kakatsa was buried alive by his mother but saved by an old woman in the tribe. Sarah and Kakatsa came with me to the kuarup ritual in Xingu Park, and I noticed how proud Kakatsa was of Sarah. The Indians loved her, and she adapted so easily to their lifestyle, even though she was a city girl from Rio. It wasn't long after our time in Xingu Park that they officially became a couple and were later married in a beautiful ceremony in Brasília in April 2009. The ceremony combined their two cultures. After the pastor's speech, Kakatsa's mother painted Sarah's forehead with red paint and hung Sarah's new hammock below Kakatsa's hammock, right behind the pulpit, symbolizing their new life together.

Their vision is to adopt several dozen children who have been rejected or abandoned. It is so powerful to see how God has redeemed their lives and used the rejection that could have killed them at birth to now give them compassion for others who have been rejected. Sarah recently gave birth to their first child, a little boy called Kaluanã, and they have adopted a girl whose mother was single and therefore knew that her father and grandfather would kill the baby.

Sarah and Kakatsa have the potential to be the future leaders of the national movement protecting the lives of the indigenous children. Kakatsa is anointed and has been given real favor with the Indians. I am no longer just a missionary to the Indians. They are my family—my daughter is Suruwahá, and my nephew is Kamaiurá!

LIFE IN CASA DAS NAÇÕES is like a small piece of heaven for me. It is so powerful to see Indians who used to be from opposing tribes living and working in harmony with each other. They spend their days growing corn and manioc and making crafts to sell as a means of sustainability. The men are studying and doing practical work on the farm.

We started an Indigenous Gastronomy Experience where people come to the Casa das Nações to have a meal prepared by the Indians. On the menu are ants in *farinha* (manioc flour) as well as other delicacies. It is an opportunity to raise awareness on the Indian lifestyle and also to make the ministry self-sustaining.

While eating ants was once such a hardship for me and I longed for pizza, I can now think of nothing better than sitting outside by the fire, watching the faces of the people I love and the children whose lives have been saved, and biting into a big, crispy ant.

God has done so much more than we could have dreamed or imagined. Since Island Breeze's 1991 visit to the Suruwahá, the overall rate of suicide has gradually decreased. Government officials report that suicide as a practice in the tribe has almost ended. Today we hear Suruwahá young men publically standing against suicide and defending the value of a long life. This was unthinkable a few decades ago.

God took the little stick I threw in the fire all those years ago and enabled Suzuki and me to be a voice for the voiceless. We know there is no greater privilege. The battle goes on, but God is in the battle, and He will have the victory.

For More Information

ATINI—VOICE FOR LIFE is a nonprofit organiza-
tion located in the federal district of Brasília. Atini works to defend the
rights of indigenous Amazonian children and families. Contact them at
voiceforlife@gmail.com.

To learn more about combating infanticide, the *Hakani* documentary,
and other organizations supporting life, visit
www.hakani.org/en/
www.voiceforlifewhoweare.blogspot.com
www.atini.org (Portuguese language)

To contact the Suzukis, visit www.suzukiemarcia.blogspot.com or e-mail
suzukiemarcia@gmail.com (Márcia)
edsonmassamiti@gmail.com (Suzuki)

Acknowledgments

I (MÁRCIA) WANT TO EXPRESS my gratitude to my loving family, especially my mother, who has always inspired me with the most beautiful and amazing combination of generosity and boldness I have ever seen. And to my father, who taught me not only how to dream, but how to pursue those dreams with perseverance and discipline. Thank you to Suzuki, whose intriguing mind and inquisitive soul always challenge me, and to the one whose radiant smile illuminates my days—my beautiful daughter Hakani.

Thank you to the indigenous peoples of Brazil, who have shared their houses, their fish, and their lives with Suzuki and me. They have granted us the most significant moments of our lives, have enriched our understanding of who God is, and have become part of our family. We deeply love and respect them.

Deepest thanks to my leader, Jim Stier, whose amazing teachings during my DTS made me understand clearly who I was and where my destiny lay. His example and loving support over the decades has inspired me to persevere "against all odds."

I am also very grateful to my sisters, Margaret and Maryangela, who have always been with me in my ministry. Their creativity, generosity, ingenuity, and willingness to make personal sacrifices to support my initiatives and to reach out to those in need are remarkable.

My profound thankfulness goes out to two people who cared for me and invested so much in my life in the context of the Methodist Church in the Amazon—Bishop Davi Ponciano and Bishop Adolfo Evaristo de Souza, my dear friends and spiritual leaders. They both have passed away and left behind a powerful testimony of faith and the pursuit of holiness.

I thank Jemimah Wright for her patience and dedication to make this book possible. You are an amazing woman of God.

Suzuki and I would like to thank the countless people who are fundamental in our life and ministry. Our pastors, friends, YWAM leaders, peers, and supporters—it is impossible to name every one. Suzuki and I have been truly humbled by your love and support over the years.

About the Authors

MÁRCIA AND EDSON SUZUKI and their daughter, Hakani, live with and minister to Amazonian tribal peoples in Brazil. Suzuki holds a master's degree in linguistics from the University of Campinas (Unicamp) in São Paulo, Brazil, and serves as a missionary of Igreja Batista do Calvario. Márcia hold a master's degree in linguistics from the Federal University of Rondônia (UNIR) in the state of Rondônia, Brazil. She serves as a missionary for the Methodist Church in the Amazon (REMA).

JEMIMAH WRIGHT is a freelance journalist and author. She studied at Oxford Brookes University, spent a year working in Cape Town, South Africa, helping to start a home for AIDS orphans, and then returned to England to train as a journalist. Jemimah has written several books for YWAM Publishing, including *Taking the High Places* and *Releasing Your Children to the Lord*. She is based in London, England. To contact her, e-mail jemimah@wrightfeatures.co.uk.

Márcia, age nine

Suruwahá round house where the Suzukis lived with the Indians

Márcia, front, traveling by canoe with Luiza, Anabel, and Vera

Márcia with a group of Suruwahá Indians in 1997. The round house is in the background.

Shaman Asia, the first Suruwahá to meet Jesus

Edson Suzuki showing the first Suruwahá dictionary to tribal children

Márcia cooking with the first clay pot she made

Hakani's brother Niawi, who was buried alive at the age of five because he could not walk or talk

Hakani's brother Bibi, who saved her life and took care of her for three years

Hakani shortly after she was given to the Suzukis. At just over five years of age, she weighed 15 pounds and measured 69 centimeters

Hakani and the Suzukis in their jungle house before traveling to the city for medical treatment

Hakani (right), six years old, next to an eight-month-old baby

Muwaji, the Suruwahá mother who fled the tribe to save the life of her daughter Iganani. The law to protect indigenous children was named after her.

Márcia and Hakani in a hammock at the Kamaiurá fishing camp, 2006

Suzuki in front of the National Congress Building in Brasília

*On the beach
at Hakani's
fourth grade
graduation,
Kona, Hawaii*

*Hakani with
Congressman
Henrique
Afonso and a
twin survivor
from the
Ticuna tribe*

*Márcia,
Congressman
Henrique
Afonso, and
the indigenous
pastor Eli
Ticuna in front
of the National
Congress
on the day
Muwaji's Law
was officially
proposed*

Hakani, the girl whose name means "smile," 2006

Hakani, Márcia, and Suzuki in Kona, 2011 (photo © Brooke Valle)

Suzuki family in Kona, 2011
(photo © Brooke Valle)